RELIGION: The Great Questions

RELIGION: The Great Questions

**DENISE LARDNER CARMODY
and JOHN CARMODY**

The Seabury Press · New York

For Kurt Reinhardt

1983
The Seabury Press
815 Second Avenue
New York, N.Y. 10017

Printed in the United States of America

Library of Congress Cataloging in Publication Data

Carmody, John, 1939-
  Religion, the great questions.

  Bibliography: p.
  Includes index.
  1. Religions.   I. Carmody, Denise Lardner,
1935-   . II. Title.
BL80.2.C344   1983   291   83-636
ISBN 0-8164-2476-4

Contents

Preface

THIS book is a modest introduction to the world religions. Its distinguishing features include a format of interlocking questions and a central byplay between Buddhism and Christianity, which we take as good representatives of the Eastern and Western traditions. By the book's end the student should have both a beginning notion of the questions that have dominated the major religious traditions, and a beginning sense of how the different traditions have fashioned their distinctive answers to these questions. Thus teachers and students using the book for formal college courses might think of it as a core text, capable of amplification through further reading in whatever direction their own particular interests suggest. For readers not enrolled in formal courses we provide an annotated bibliography, whose readings indicate the next level of study for all the traditions we treat.

Our thanks to Avery Brooke and Jack Whelan of Seabury Press, who proposed the project; to Karla Kraft of the Religion Department at Wichita State University, who typed the manuscript expertly; and to Stefanie Johnson, who prepared the glossary.

Introduction

WHAT IS RELIGION?

If you look at the religion page of a typical American newspaper, you will find mainly listings of services, lectures, and social activities. Most of the listings will pertain to Christian churches, a few to Jewish synagogues, and in urban areas a scattering to Eastern groups. Thus your impression likely will be that "religion" is something social: a sharing of ideas, convictions, symbols, or ceremonies by which a group of people situates itself in the world, talks to itself about what is important in life, or rallies itself to acts of social service.

That is not a bad description of religion. Almost all of religion, historically, has referred to groups, and a great deal of religion has taken institutional forms. Nonetheless, religion is not just another cultural phenomenon, alongside education and banking. What people do in churches, synagogues, or mosques is not the whole of religion, and the questions that religion deals with have a special significance for all of a culture's activities.

The social side of religion is not the whole because, as Alfred North Whitehead saw, religion is also what people do in solitude.[1] The questions with which religion deals have a special significance for all of a culture's activities because, as Paul Tillich saw, religion is the inmost source of culture, its core significance.[2] Thus we have to move religion beyond the churches and synagogues. The solitary work of many poets and scientists carries religious implications, as do the solitary sufferings of many people not active in any religious group. The deepest myths and symbols of any

1

culture bear religious significance, even a culture such as that of the USSR which proclaims itself atheistic.

In our view, religion is the dimension of human life that deals with ultimate questions. The great issues of where we came from, where we are going, and what we ought to live for comprise religion's living heart. Insofar as such issues are inseparable from an examined life, religion is at the center of human reflection. Thus it is hard to conceive of a person or group having become mature without having struggled with religious questions. Indeed, there is an important sense in which religion is part and parcel of human authenticity. If a person pays attention to experience, strives to be intelligent, tries to be judicious, and struggles to act responsibly, he or she is accomplishing the basic programs of both human authenticity and genuine religion. The authenticity will manifest itself as an honesty, a goodness, an integrity that make the person ring true. The religion will manifest itself as an openness to the mysteriousness that attention, intelligence, good judgment, and responsibility find all sectors of human life to carry.

This mysteriousness is the heart of the religious matter. In nature, society, and the self the dynamics of human authenticity come upon a fullness, a silence, a "more" that stop the mind and invite the heart to trust. What is the source of the matter that has evolved into the universe we now perceive? How can human beings produce both so much good and so much evil? Where can my self find rest? These questions have no factual, empirically certain answers. They take us to a point of view, a dimension of reality, where we sense there is more than we can comprehend. Our minds, which seem made to handle material things, come face to face with the spiritual issue of a whole. As a result, we are confused, uncomfortable, even irritated. Religion is not business as usual. Genuine religion is intercourse with the mystery of our beginning, our depths, and our term.

For this reason, the religious traditions (which we may see as so many ways of dealing with life's basic mystery) regularly focus on conversion. We must be converted, turned around, if we are to embark on a serious religious life. Business as usual shies away from questions of life's beginning, depth, and final term. Such questions detract from selling products, making money, running a home. Spend too much time on them and you'll find yourself a misfit, no longer comfortable with your fellow workers or even your own family. Ironically, the more you pursue life's ultimate questions as though they were personally significant, the less you will please even the average church or college.

Mystery puts all ordinary business and thought in brackets. So religion is always in tension with ordinary life. Ordinary life depends on religion to give it direction and purpose, yet religion can upset ordinary life in a flash. If we become fanatical about religion we can ruin ordinary culture, yet if we neglect religion ordinary culture will turn to stone. Very strange and very potent, this activity called religion.

To consort with mystery, life's ultimate questions and powers, is to find ordinary consciousness a sort of dreaming. Once wakened to the omnipresence of mystery, of what the West has called God, a person is never quite the same. Thenceforth the rest of society seems a bit crazy, but nature becomes a more congenial home. Fellow seekers become special friends, but the ease with which religious people lose psychic balance makes one tread lightly, go in humble garb.

WHY SHOULD WE STUDY RELIGION?

If religion is essentially dealing with the mysteriousness of life that the ultimate questions of our origin, depth, and destiny reveal, it remains to be shown that studying religion is profitable. In our opinion studying religion is not profitable, if one's notion of profit is mainly financial. Nothing in this book is going to add a penny to your bank account, but quite a bit of it is going to challenge the great value that secular American culture places on money. On the other hand, studying religion should clarify a number of the happenings that fill your daily newspaper, and it may also clarify a number of your own inner confusions.

Let us deal first with the happenings reported in the newspapers. Consider, for instance, the turmoil that has become routine in the Middle East. In addition to the basic issues of a homeland for the Palestinians and the assurance of Israel's survival, religious factors beg a sober assessment. For example, many of the Israeli settlers on the West Bank belong to devout, if not fundamentalist religious groups who look upon "Judea" and "Samaria" as given to them by God, part of their biblical heritage.[3] On the other side, Muslims the world over look upon Jerusalem as one of their holiest cities, the site of the revered mosque of the Dome of the Rock, so they vow not to rest until at least East Jerusalem returns to Muslim control. Christians also have a vested interest in the government of Jerusalem, because Jerusalem is the city where their savior died and was raised, and Christian faith is an important factor in the related turmoils of Lebanon, which has long struggled to harmonize Christians with Muslims.

Nor do the religious factors lessen if one expands one's study of the Middle East and becomes more comprehensive. The conflicts between Iran and several other Muslim countries, most notably Iraq, are in part the product of the historical antagonisms between Iran's *Shiite* version of

Islam and other countries' *Sunni* version, while much of the opposition to the Soviet invasion of Afghanistan has come from devout Islamic tribes who fiercely desire a Muslim political regime. The large ethical questions that the conflicts of the Middle East raise, such as the morality of the terrorist tactics of the PLO and the destructive responses of the Israelis, the morality of the huge arms sales of the United States and the Soviet Union, and the morality of the outside powers' willingness to pursue Middle Eastern oil by military means, also take one into the region of religion. None of these ethical questions can be settled satisfactorily without considering such religious matters as the biblical commandment not to kill, the traditional Jewish and Muslim views of how to secure social justice, the traditional Christian teaching that property rights are more public than private, and many religions' sense that all human beings stand as equals before the throne of God.[4]

One could make similar analyses of recent news reports about Poland, Northern Ireland, or the antinuclear movement in Western Europe and the United States, showing that until we understand the religious factors in these situations our picture of them is bound to remain clouded. Simply factually, religion weaves its way through our economics, sociology, history, and psychology, frequently functioning as a very powerful force. Therefore, not to have at least a modest acquaintance with the main religious traditions and issues is to be ignorant about a great deal, present happenings every bit as much as past.

So much for the news reports that fill the papers. But what about your own inner confusions? "Those are none of your business," you may well say, and your saying has a lot to commend it. It is not the proper function of academic religious studies to preach, proselytize, or propagandize, turning professors into clergy. On the other hand, the subject matter of religion by its very nature frequently is personal or existential, since it concerns views of reality that profess to be able to change a whole life.

Our solution to the problem this raises is to try to walk a middle line. We certainly are not going to preach to you, nor argue on behalf of any of the religious traditions we present. What you make of the personal implications these traditions' teachings carry will be completely your own affair. On the other hand, we are not going to downplay the personal relevance that the teachings themselves clearly may have. To understand why the Buddha has been so important in Asian history, you have to grasp the problem many Asians have thought the Buddha solved and the great freedom his solution has given them. The only way to grasp this problem firmly is to see its occurrence in your own life. Until you have confronted your own sufferings and vividly imagined how the removal of desire might gut them, you will not appreciate the Buddha, Buddhism, the peace Asia has pursued, or what passion means to every human being's struggle for happiness.

That's our middle line: no preaching, but no backing away from the personal implications a given religious teaching may carry. As you may have noted, we never even consider the possibility that you have no inner confusions and so are not a good candidate for religious studies. Were we to assume that we would seriously shortchange you, not letting you be human like we are, reducing you to the dimensions you have on Wall Street or where they make video games. For us, you are immensely more than what you buy and how you may be distracted. If the religions hold any truth at all, a central part of you always wonders about greater questions.

HOW SHOULD WE STUDY RELIGION?

In sketching why we should study religion, we have already indicated much of the *how*. For example, the significance of religion the world over implies that we should study religion with an internationalist, worldwide point of view. Certainly today's interlocking economic, ecological, and political systems are producing something close to a global culture, so it will not do to limit our study to the religious traditions that flourish here at home. If we are to understand either our own times or the history that led up to them, we will have to appreciate the religious backgrounds of Indians and Chinese, Japanese and Africans, as well as those of Europeans and North Americans.

Moreover, there is a dictum in religious studies that the person who knows only one religion knows no religion. "Religion" is an umbrella, and you cannot grasp its significance until you know what it covers. So long as you know only what "God" signifies in Christian terms, you will miss the impersonal, naturalistic overtones that divinity has carried in the East. So long as you only think of prayer in biblical categories, you will miss the religious significance of Eastern meditation.

Second, the significance of the ultimate questions at religion's core implies that we should study religion with a special sensitivity to the problems it tries to solve. True, these problems are more than conceptual, so we have to understand "questions" as more than intellectual inquiries. Granted that, however we can learn a great deal about religion and human nature by attending to the ways that religious doctrines, symbols, rituals, and the like represent efforts to deal with suffering, evil, death, the need for group coherence, the need for sacral play, and other deep human concerns. To be sure, there is a surplus, gratuitous side to religion, where it is less a matter of meeting human needs and more a matter of appreciating mystery's unexpected splendors, but meeting human needs is the backbone of many religious enterprises. Thus our study should pay special attention to what John Bowker has called the "compound of limitations" that religion would help us fathom.[5] In evolutionary perspective, religion is a major way that human beings have tried to break through the prisons in which death, evil, and other forms of limitation might otherwise have kept them.

Third, in addition to being internationalist and question-oriented, our study should be academic. In contrast to the proselytizing or special pleading that can characterize studies of religion in the churches or synagogues, we want a study that grants all the traditions equal status. The approach to religion that most college courses now take is evenhanded in this way. Contrasting itself with a *theological* approach, in which one's faith sets the horizon in terms of which one views other religions, the academic approach brackets questions of the investigator's own ultimate allegiance and simply tries to let the various traditions speak for themselves. Students finally must decide which traditions they prefer, but it is not the part of the professor to tilt the game. Unless Taoist or Buddhist or Jewish views get a fair hearing, one never will know why they have proven useful to so many people through the centuries, or how they might enrich even non-Taoists, non-Buddhists, and non-Jews today.

Fourth, as we said in the previous section, this concern not to preach but to keep an academic detachment does not mean that we should blunt the personal implications that the teachings of the religious traditions may carry. A liberal education is above all concerned with freeing the individual student from the constraints in which ignorance, prejudice, or an unchallenged culture would keep him, so presenting the personal implications of the different religions' positions is completely in keeping with the canons of liberal education. Moreover, it is completely in keeping with the way that people best learn, for the best learning occurs when people are involved, passionate, concerned to make knowledge bear on the confusions afflicting their own inmost selves. In a word, significant and creative human learning is *personal*, as Michael Polanyi eloquently demonstrated a quarter of a century ago.[6]

Thus our methodological or pedagogical approach stands foursquare: a concentation on religion's worldwide span of traditions, a stress on religion's orientation toward profound human questions, an objective or academic approach that pleads for no one religious tradition in particular, and a stress on the personal implications of the religious traditions' teachings that should help students sense how relevant many adherents of the traditions have found those teachings to be.

People who like to correlate pedagogy with the established academic disciplines might tie our concentration on the worldwide span of the religious traditions to history. Similarly, they might tie our stress on religion's concern with ultimate questions to philosophy. Our effort to preserve an academic detachment while retaining religion's personal thrust suggests a theory of knowledge such as that of Bernard Lonergan, in which objectivity and subjectivity finally are two sides of the same coin.[7] Last, our need to take up sociological, psychological, and ecological issues will suggest why current departments of religion usually encourage a variety of disciplinary approaches.[8]

HOW IS THIS BOOK GOING TO PROCEED?

To put these pedagogical goals into concrete form, we have structured this book around four major questions. Part One is concerned with the human quest, humanity's general effort to make sense of its experience and so come to a measure of peace and prosperity. This quest or search or adventure has preoccupied all the major traditions, several of which have described themselves as a "way." For example, early Christians described faith in Jesus as "the way," Buddhists have long described the teaching of the Enlightened One as "the middle way," and Taoists take their name from the "way" (tao) of nature that moves the ten thousand things comprising reality. We begin, then, with some representative religious views of the human quest, humanity's search for a way to go well through time and tide.

More specifically, Part One asks several questions that break the general problem of the human quest into important subfoci: For what are human beings searching? Of what use is Jesus (or Buddha, or the paradigm of some other religious tradition) in clarifying this search? How may we hope to grow? What do we owe one another? How should we finally conceive the reality in the midst of which God, the ultimate, or fate has placed us? In explaining how a given religious tradition responds to these subquestions, we will be describing that tradition's general slant on the human quest. Your job will be to try to grasp this general slant or point of view and then ask what light it sheds on your own human quest.

Part Two deals with the problem of evil, a staple concern in all the religious traditions. For a subfocus of the problem of evil we first take the question of how we should view nature, the source of such evils as earthquakes and cancers. Then we deal with the sociopolitical question of why states fail to flourish and the personal or psychological question of what makes human beings sad. Our fourth question is how we should regard death, which is a problem (if not an evil) afflicting us in spirit as well as body, and our fifth question is what the given tradition considers to be the greatest evil, the polar opposite of its highest good.

Part Three focuses on God, the supreme being or ultimate reality that has played a major role in many of the world religions. First we ask what the given tradition means by this word "God," since the traditions vary considerably in their understanding of the term. Then we ask where God is in our lives. This leads to the question of whether there is a privileged way to God and, fourth, to the question of how we should understand religious rituals. The last question in Part Three deals with ethics, the behavior that God seems to require.

Part Four is entitled "The Good Life." Its subfoci are how we ought to work, what is good sexual love, why we should pray, how we can achieve social justice, and how we may become friends of the earth. The first two of these questions recall Freud's notion that good mental health requires the ability to love and to work. The third question moves beyond Freud, to the notion that ultimate reality may be inviting us to interpersonal dealings. Question four draws on the currently influential school of liberation theology, which has placed the issue of social justice high on all the religions' agendas.[9] Question five comes from the ecological crisis and environmentalist movement, which make it clear that unless we become reconciled to nature the earth's whole future will be imperiled.

In each of these parts, we deal with three of the world religious traditions, trying to answer the five subfocal questions as we think these traditions would. Thus, in Part One we deal with the human quest from a Christian, a Buddhist, and a Hindu point of view. In Part Two we poll Taoists, Buddhists, and Christians for their views of evil. Part Three represents Buddhist, Muslim, and Christian views of God. For Part Four, on the good life, our representative traditions are Christianity, Judaism, and Buddhism.

Overall, we deal with three traditions that generally are considered Eastern (Buddhism, Hinduism, Taoism,) and three traditions that generally are considered Western (Christianity, Islam, Judaism). However, in order to facilitate a deeper look at both Eastern and Western religion, and a deeper comparison between the two, we have dealt with Buddhism and Christianity in each Part. We could have used other representatives of either the East or the West, but Buddhism and Christianity seem the best overall candidates, in view of our readers' likely backgrounds and interests, and in view of our own sense that the dialogue between Buddhists and Christians may well be the wave of the *ecumenical* future.

From time to time throughout the individual chapter sections, in the

Part Introductions, and in our Conclusion we take note of other religious traditions, such as Confucianism, Shinto, and the ancient convictions of nonliterate groups. We also take note of professedly irreligious traditions such as Marxism. The result, we hope, will be a fairly comprehensive introduction to the ways that people the world over have responded to the great questions which life's mysteriousness has set them.

PART ONE

The Human Quest

T HE Greek philosopher Aristotle taught that we begin the life that is in love with wisdom when we first *wonder*. Until something strikes us as wonderful, intriguing, we are stuck in second gear, putt-putting along the back roads of human potential. However, let us really see a flower or a deer or a soul and our humanity starts to race. After an initial moment of wordless wonder, silent admiration, we want to understand. How do flowers grow into such effortless perfection? What musculature gives a deer its ineffable grace? Why do certain human beings turn ordinary experiences into sweet friendship or dazzling art?

The examined life, the religious life, is but the sustaining of questions such as these. Pursuing them into the mysterious source of flowers, deer, and souls, we come upon divinity or Tao. Reflecting on their implications for ourselves, the ways we might change our dispersions of money or time, we come upon the *mystery* of our own depths, which St. Augustine called "more intimate to me than I am to myself." Letting ourselves follow the dispositions of awe, reverence, and gratitude that this mystery tends to elicit, we start to become formally, explicitly religious: people who worship or pray.

These are but a few of the modalities that the human quest for meaning, peace, and prosperity can take. The world over, most human beings have employed them. For example, if we take the most probable significance of the remains that prehistoric people have left us, we find that the earliest members of our species were religious: reverent toward the powers they thought presided over life and death.[1] Because these powers held the key to a sucessful hunt, prehistoric peoples probably honored them with songs

11

and dances begging that the hunt go well. Because these powers were the people's final recourse in times of sickness and death, the people probably honored them in rites designed to ward off sickness and pacify the dead. Since human fertility was most prominent in women, who grew great with child and issued forth new life, prehistoric people carved statues of pregnant figures, suggesting that the ultimate powers were like a mother to the earth or took a special presence in female fertility.

The gap between ourselves and these people who lived tens of thousands of years ago lessens considerably when we realize that modern human beings still wonder about the things that matter most. For instance, while we moderns have developed an impressive array of information about human reproduction, now being able to accomplish it with stored semen and borrowed wombs, new human life itself remains mysterious, as anyone who has held an infant is likely to testify. The egg and sperm one can see through a microscope are totally different from an infant. Indeed, Whittaker Chambers, the prime witness against the famous spy Alger Hiss, was brought to his knees and religious faith by the perfection of his child's tiny ear. That he should behold such perfection, when nine months before there had been almost nothing at all, cried out for praise and thanksgiving.

Much the same applies to the experience of death, which also has not changed essentially in tens of thousands of years. We still know nothing about where our dead parents or friends "go." We still don't understand the necessity that all living things must die. Modern science has doubled the average human life span, but each of us still lives but a few seconds of the earth's allotted day. So, as much as our earliest human forebears, we spend our years under the shadow of mortality. Like theirs, our quests must tramp the road to death. As the philosopher Martin Heidegger put it, the human being is being-unto-death. Until we come to terms with our mortality, and move out to the comprehensive Being that may give it adequate perspective, we flee the wisdom of our bones, neglect the consolation in our blood.

Part One plays off these fundamental aspects of the human quest, focusing on some of the questions the religious traditions themselves have chosen to feature. Granted human mortality, what does Christian or Buddhist or Hindu wisdom say that human beings are searching for? Granted human beings' searching, what use is Jesus, the Buddha, or Hindu revelation? If searching is our fate, how can we turn searching into an adventure, an opportunity to flex our spirits and grow? If we are all condemned to search, all are mortal and want to grow, what do we owe one another, how might we be allies? Finally, how should we conceive the comprehensive reality in the midst of which we search and struggle? What world view best factors the primal zones (nature, society, the self, and divinity) that the classical human quests have discovered?

Through these questions, we hope to show you central aspects of the Christian, Buddhist, and Hindu traditions, and central aspects of human beings throughout history, from the earliest Ice Age to the latest today. We could easily formulate other good questions, but the troubles of these will suffice for today. The most important effect our questions will have, if they are working upon you as we hope they will, will be to move you into a stable disposition to wonder. It is this stable disposition, rather than any of our particular inquiries, that will set you before the mystery that the religions have called their origin and life.

ONE

A Christian View

FOR WHAT ARE HUMAN BEINGS SEARCHING?

Christianity is ancient enough in its mythic structure (in the psychic depths from which its main story comes) to focus the human quest on the axial issues of life and death. However, as we shall see with other religious traditions, the understanding of "life" and "death" becomes both multi-leveled and paradoxical. The life that Christianity claims human beings are searching for, and the death that Christianity claims human beings are struggling to avoid, are spiritual even more than physical. Taking the story of Jesus as their cue, Christians came to believe that the fullest human life stems from union with God, the Holy Spirit of love. In their view, this life brings a peace and joy that fulfill the human being as nothing else can. As well, it brings comfort and strength in the midst of the sufferings that human mortality and evil inevitably carry in their train. At the limit, the life of the Christian God defeats death and evil, resurrecting those whom it fills and placing them definitively with a God who (as the Eastern Orthodox Christian liturgy loves to sing) is holy, mighty, and immortal.

Let us unpack this summary set of propositions. Christianity began with Jesus of Nazareth, a devout Jew. Most of Jesus' religious convictions came from his Jewish tradition, especially his conviction that God, the creator of the world, is active and loving. In the exodus, when Moses led the Hebrews out of Egypt, Hebrew faith had long seen a special sign of God's helpful activity. In the covenant that God made with them through Moses, the Hebrews had come to feel themselves especially bonded to the Holy One. The innovations that Jesus made in this tradition went in the direction of personalizing God's love and care. In place of "Lord," Jesus tended to call God "Father" (Abba). For Jesus, the creator of the world and deliverer of Israel was as close and trustworthy as a loving father.[1]

Jesus preached that God was making available to any who wished it an intimate relation like that of a parent to a child. The kingdom or reign of God, as Jesus called it, was the new era of peace, justice, and rightness that this intimate relation could produce. Where people had felt alienated from God, because of God's distance and their own transgressions, God the Father would convince them that his love was both near and capable of giving them a new start. Where people had felt alienated from one another, strangers or enemies or competitors, God the Father would convince them that they were children of the same parent, branches of a single vine.

The "proof" that Jesus offered for these convictions boiled down to his own intriguing life. The words that he spoke were new, fresh, an overflow of his intense connection to the Father. The works that he performed were signs that God's love could heal bodies and cure souls. Even the opposition that his preaching raised became for his followers a sign of confirmation. Those who clung to the status quo, who sought security in money or power, had to oppose the new kingdom of God, because it shone light into their selfish darkness, forced justice into their squalid back rooms.

So his followers believed that Jesus died because he roused the forces of evil, and that he was resurrected because his Father's love smashed the forces of evil and death. By faith in Jesus, a follower could open him- or herself to Jesus' sort of relation with God, becoming a child of the divine Abba as Jesus had been. By participating in the life of worship and service that Jesus' followers led, a convert could take on Jesus' mind, experience in his heart the Holy Spirit whom Jesus had known. And, like Jesus, the follower would be moved by this new life to a union with God that carried across the grave. In "heaven," a state of ultimate fulfillment, Christians believed that the follower would enjoy the full flowering of God's love, coming to know with something of the divine understanding, love with something of the divine love, and share the splendor of God with myriad sisters and brothers.

For Christianity, then, human beings are searching for heaven, a completely fulfilling union with God. Eye has not seen, nor ear heard, nor the heart of any human being fully conceived what heaven entails, but the mainstream of the Christian tradition has been convinced that it would be full light for the mind and full love for the heart. Emphasizing the heart, the fourth-century "father" St. Augustine declaimed: "You have made us for yourself, O Lord, and our hearts are restless till they rest in You." Emphasizing the mind, the thirteenth-century "doctor" St. Thomas taught that heaven essentially would be the beatific vision of God—the unmediated perception of the only One who could make sense of the plurality of creation. Emphasizing social justice, many contemporary Christian theologians translate heaven as the state in which human beings would live as genuine equals, neither oppressing nor being oppressed.

Whatever the particular figure, each age of Christianity has believed in, hoped for, and loved to anticipate a condition of complete fulfillment. God himself would be the substance of this complete fulfillment, ravishing the human spirit in holy love, but heaven would touch all aspects of human existence, bodily and socially as well as spiritual. Thus in the Christian view of the human quest, the term we seek is not too strange, but too good.

OF WHAT USE IS JESUS CHRIST?

In developing their views of human fulfillment, Christians have above all depended upon the example of Jesus. Because of the sublimity of his message, the power of his deeds, and the unheard of intervention by God in his resurrection, Jesus became for his followers the "Christ," the anointed one or messiah. This meant that he was God's special messenger and agent of deliverance, the bringer of salvation. Through Jesus God had worked the ground-level liberation that human beings seek: freedom from death and evil, entry into loving union with God and one another. Jesus had manifested God's power, proclaimed God's saving intent, and given his own life for the fulfillment of God's plan. In all ways, therefore, he was his followers' central reason for faith, the alpha and omega of their religion.[2]

As time went on and Christians pondered the significance of Jesus more deeply, they developed a Christology (an understanding of Jesus' messiahship) that went well beyond the prior Jewish conceptions. By the end of the apostolic era, when those who had known Jesus personally had all died out and the New Testament scriptures were essentially complete, Jesus stood forth as both the exemplar of human authenticity and the privileged revelation of God. If one wanted to know how to live a holy life, Jesus was the first model. His love of God and love of neighbor had perfectly fulfilled his own twofold command: "You shall love the Lord your God with all your heart, and with all your soul, and with all your mind. This is the great and first commandment. And a second is like it, You shall love your neighbor as yourself" (Matthew 22:37–39).

In fulfilling this twofold command of love, Jesus had definitively revealed what God is like. As Christian faith developed, this revelation led to a confession that Jesus *was* God, partook of the very divine nature. For the greatest theologians of the New Testament, Paul and John, Jesus was the Son or Word of God who had existed from the beginning, as long as God had been God. The followers of Paul developed Paul's convictions about Jesus' divinity into a lovely hymn about the Word's function in creation: "In him all things were created, in heaven and on earth, visible and invisible, whether thrones or dominions or principalities or authorities—all things were created through him and for him. He is before all things, and in him all things hold together." (Colossians 1:16–17) The Gospel of John bluntly states John's convictions at the very head of the book: "In the beginning was the Word, and the Word was with God, and the Word was God. He was in the beginning with God; all things were made through him, and without him was not anything made that was made" (John 1:1–3).

Thus it would have been somewhat misleading to ask about the "use" of Jesus Christ. In his followers' eyes, he had served God's plan of revelation and salvation, but not really as an instrument or tool. Rather, Jesus had revealed what God is like because Jesus himself had derived from God, possessed the divine nature. When this question came into sharp focus, during the debates of the early fourth century that culminated in the Council of Nicaea (325), the bishops came down on the side of Jesus' strict divinity: He was *consubstantial* (of the same substance) with the Father. Indeed, only this strict divinity had made it possible for Jesus to save human beings from sin and unite them with God. Through the Incarnation, the Word had taken a full humanity up into identity with God. As St. Athanasius, one of the leading bishops at Nicaea, put it: What was not assumed was not saved. Had Jesus not joined a full humanity to his own divinity as the Word, humanity would still stand alienated from God.

So Christians came not so much to use Jesus as to gaze upon him as the icon of their God. East and West, they read the gospels as the story of the sojourn of the divine Son upon earth, the living miracle of God's Word having come into time and pitched his tent among us. God's only motive in this great condescension was divine love and mercy. Nothing utilitarian moved the Master of the Universe, only his own goodness. Once and for all, Jesus stood in the world of space and time as the blazing proof of God's goodness. "God so loved the world that he gave his only Son, that whoever believes in him should not perish but have eternal life" (John 3:16). No greater love could even God show, than to lay down his beloved's life for the sake of making us human beings friends.

For Christian faith, insofar as we hunger to know and love such a good God, living with him forever in heaven, Jesus specifies or concretizes our great grounds for gladness. Insofar as we have always tended to turn our backs on this good God, and to hurt one another grievously, Jesus specifies or concretizes the evil in us, our sinful refusal to love. From the cross,

Jesus preaches that only by the stripes of his Son was God able to heal the deep wounds of human sin. Shining with the light of the resurrection, Jesus preaches that where sin abounded grace has abounded the more, since God is always greater than our hearts, even when our hearts condemn us as evil. Thus the passover of Jesus from death to resurrection has stood in history as humanity's great crux. For Christians, Jesus crucified and risen comforts the afflicted, but afflicts the comfortable. Look at him squarely, Christians have said, and your life can never be what it was.

HOW MAY WE HOPE TO GROW?

For traditional Christian faith, we may hope to grow dialectically, back and forth, sometimes being comforted and sometimes being afflicted. When we are down, depressed by the torpor in ourselves or oppressed by the evil in the world, the God whom Jesus called the Holy Spirit serves as our comforter. The light has shone in the darkness, the Spirit reminds us, and the darkness has not overcome it. There could not be this world, let alone this world's hardy band of saints, were there not a God much stronger than chaos, much more creative than human machinations. Indeed, why is there something, a creation, at all? None of us explains her or his own being—nor do her parents, or the first primates, or the first molecules of hydrogen. Each of these is finite, limited, changing—a fusion of being and nothingness. Without a powerful God, there would be only nothingness. In the Christian view, creation is precisely *ex nihilo:* from the void that alone opposes God. Since there are being, goodness, and love (however much they are imperiled), there must be an unassailable, self-sufficient source of being, goodness, and love. Traditionally, that is how the Christian mind has ascended to God.

The Holy Spirit also comforts those slashed and bruised by human evils. Terrible as their incursions may be, human evils need not corrupt the human soul. According to Christian conviction, they can kill the body, warp the psyche, take most of the joy out of life, but they cannot force the human spirit to violate itself, come to call evil good. Tiny as this little zone of freedom may seem, it has stood against some of the world's most impressive tyrannies. Indeed as the Russian writer Alexsandr Solzhenitsyn showed in his eloquent Nobel Lecture on Literature, what the world's worst tyrannies finally most fear is the poet's or the scientist's or the simple citizen's unflinching little word of truth.[3]

Whenever evil, failure, or just fatigue threaten to plow us under, the Spirit of God offers comfort, like a nursing mother rocking and crooning to her child. We need only let go, cast ourselves upon the waters, and something much greater than we will start to buoy us up. Indeed, this something much greater will take over the prayer of our hearts, so that God will begin to speak up for us to God: "Likewise the Spirit helps us in our weakness; for we do not know how to pray as we ought, but the Spirit himself intercedes for us with sighs too deep for words. And he who searches the hearts of men knows what is the mind of the Spirit, because the Spirit intercedes for the saints according to the will of God" (Romans 8:26–27).

Thus, the overall Christian understanding of our human pilgrimage assigns a primacy to *grace*. Grace is God's favor, God's benevolence, God's self-offer, love, and aid. No matter where our twisting and turning may take us, we are preceded by, supported by, lured by an ultimate mystery that wishes us well. For no merits of our own, simply because God is Love (1 John 4:8), history is tilted in our favor. "For I am sure that neither death, nor life, nor angels, nor principalities, nor things present, nor things to come, nor powers, nor height, nor depth, nor anything else in all creation will be able to separate us from the love of God in Christ Jesus our Lord" (Romans 8:38–39)—because that's the way Jesus showed, proved, promised God always would be.

The key to our growth, in Christian terms, is our willingness daily to put faith in this sort of God to the test. Only empirically, by trial and error, can we learn what grace does and does not mean. For example, if we test the goodness of God, relying upon it and using it as our touchstone, we will find before long that it does not shield us from ordinary pains or challenges. We still have to learn discipline, feed our minds, put up with thoughtless neighbors, see our time, money, and faith wasted by society's corruptions. God never promised us a pink Cadillac, let alone a rose garden of untroubled peace. The more we try to follow the Spirit in prayer, to walk in Jesus' ways, the more aware we become of our own selfishness, of the world's injustices, of the havoc being wreaked on God's good creation. The nations' rush to war and destruction assumes the proportions of sacrilegious madness. Our own rush to comfort and distraction assume the proportions of pamperedness and sloth.

Increasingly, therefore, we find our softness and self-centeredness afflicted. Christians are convinced God will not let us think grace is cheap or maturity comes easily. The cross of Christ, God's excruciating way of saving us from sin, must start to become personally significant. The only way radically to overcome evil, Jesus' example shouts, is to absorb evil into a stronger love. The hatred that his enemies thrust upon him Jesus absorbed into his more powerful love. The cowardice of his closest followers he absorbed into his more powerful love. Even the dereliction that the Christian scriptures record (Matthew 27:46, Mark 15:34) proved less powerful than Jesus' surpassing love of his Father, whose will was his meat and drink.

These are not comforting thoughts to contemplate. According to Christianity, we must become far better than most of us now want to be. God wants *all* our love (whole mind, heart, soul, and strength) and so sanctions no self-indulgence. Our neighbors are exactly our equals, and so *deserve* the shirt from our backs. We and the world *can* grow to peace and prosperity, if we will love this much. That is the disturbing Christian proposition.

WHAT DO WE OWE ONE ANOTHER?

If we are exactly on a par before God, equally assured of the divine love and equally drawn by the Spirit to put on the mind of Christ, what do we owe one another? In terms of respect and support, how does Christianity view the social side of the human quest?[4]

For Christianity, sociology is largely a function of ecclesiology. The Christian Church (*ecclesia*) is the gathering or assembly of those who make Jesus the guide of their quest. Jesus therefore is the primary recipient of the Christian's allegiance, but the relation between Jesus and his followers puts the followers in an intimate union with one another. Two figures predominate in the New Testament descriptions of this union. One is the Pauline figure of the body of Christ (e.g., 1 Corinthians 12:12–31). The other is the Johannine figure of the vine and the branches (John 15:1–11).

Both figures are organic, saying that Christians share a common life. The union among Jesus' believers is vital, living, because Jesus and the Spirit are intensely alive. The Pauline figure deals with incorporation. Believers become part of an extended "body" of Christ, through the incorporating act of baptism. Going down with Jesus, dying to sin, they arise to a new communal life. Thereafter they are members of Christ, Christ's bodily "parts," and members of one another. Just as a human body's different members play different roles, but are all important to the total body's well-being, so the different members of Christ's mystical body play different roles but are all important in God's total scheme. Thus at the core of the New Testament's sociology is what today we might call a healthy pluralism. If people share a common allegiance, agree on a central treasure such as Christ, they are free to develop various gifts or play different roles. Not all have to be prophets, calling their times to account. Some can be patient teachers, laying foundations for the long haul, or custodial administrators, caring for mundane matters day by day. If the many members appreciate their collaborative situation, recognize their mutual need, they will treat one another kindly, supportively, as people who really share a common life.

The Johannine figure stresses abiding in Christ. The faith, hope, and love (the "theological virtues") that the Holy Spirit nurtures in believers' hearts are the vital substance of John's sociology. It is by being in love with Jesus, and through Jesus with the Father, Son, and Spirit, that people become the organic "cooperative" God intends them to be. They should love one another, because their first instinct should be to express their gratitude for the extraordinary fact that God has first loved them. They should account themselves equally humble, for they should realize that apart from the vine none of the branches can bear fruit. And they should deal gently with one another's weaknesses, because they should recall Jesus' words that the branches must be pruned, if they are to bear the fullest fruit. Only by suffering life's inevitable afflictions, which can purify their faith, hope, and love, will the members of the Christian assembly become what their God wants them to be. Only by sacrifice will they so love one another that the world may believe God has sent his only begotten Son to save it (John 17:21–23).

Historically, this ecclesiology has prompted Christians to say that human beings owe one another a great deal. The pilgrimage people share is from, by, and toward the same God, so all people are essentially brothers and sisters. Minimally, we owe one another an honest enactment of this familial relationship. Minimally, we owe one another honesty, justice, and love. So, for example, the early Church fathers and classical theologians taught that no human being has the right to superfluities as long as any human being lacks necessities. The goods of the earth are for all the earth's people. All the earth's people are so essentially equal that for one to want seriously while another waxes fat is a grievous sin before God.

In the view of critical observers, Christians have usually downplayed this radical sociology. Distinguishing between insiders and outsiders, they have often consigned "pagans," nonbelievers, to an inferior status, opening the doors to pogroms, ghettos, and rapacious colonialisms. Unable to keep their own house in order, they have fragmented the body of Christ, sundered the many branches, through a shocking history of heresies, schisms, and injustices. In flagrant violation of the commandment given them in John 17, where Jesus is remembered as having enjoined his followers to unity, they have snarled and clawed and bitten, at the extreme even burning one another at the stake. The two great divisions of the Body of Christ, the East-West schism of the eleventh century and the Catholic-Protestant split of the sixteenth century, are but the worst chapters in a general history that puts all the churches to shame. Those who could have shared the very life of God chose to hate one another for nonessentials. No wonder they have so little credibility in the modern world.

Still, a chastened Christian believer might say that although the servants have played their roles very badly, the master continues to preach good news. Despite the depressing record of his followers, Jesus' hopes for human beings, Jesus' radical sociology, keeps challenging all the members of our human tribe. God wills our unity, Jesus says, and what God wills God gives the strength to accomplish. We need not hold one another in nuclear, economic, social, or sexual bondage. Had we the wit and courage to open our hearts, we could be a happy family, a species peaceful and prosperous.

HOW SHOULD WE CONCEIVE REALITY?

For Christians, human torpor is a serious problem. Why do we not do the good that we should do? Why do we do the evil that we should not do? We take up this problem fully in Part Two, but it deserves at least passing mention here. When the Christian has looked upon the world, he has seen a creation that Genesis says God called good, a history that the New Testament says Christ has redeemed, and the detritus of human beings' persistent failure to appropriate these sayings. The result has been a somewhat sophisticated interpretation of "reality."

In the beginning, at the foundations of the world, the good God chose to create. This choice brought God no advantage, for there was nothing wanting to God. The motive for creation was only God's desire to communicate the divine being and contentedness. So the inmost significance of creation, the witness it shouts just by being, is the glory of the good God who made it. Among the books of the Christian Old Testament, the Psalms stand out for this message. Above all, the Psalms sing praise to God the creator and redeemer, above all they extoll the splendor of the Master of the Universe.[5] The lives of human beings, they say, are essentially given for worship. From the sun's rising in the east to its setting in the west, human beings should see the world as a cause for giving praise to God.

But most human beings do not look upon the world this way, and the inhumanity of their fellows is a large part of the reason why they do not. In the main, their fellows shield themselves from a rising of the sun that would begin the day with thanksgiving, from a setting of the sun that would conclude the day with contrition. Cut off from a heavenly perspective, from the imperatives of the Kingdom of God, most human beings shrink their quest to the business of making a living.

Still, we should not exaggerate the irreligion of our contemporaries, as though past societies overflowed with piety and justice. Almost four thousand years ago an unknown Egyptian poet composed a dispute between a man contemplating suicide and the man's better self or soul. When the man explains why he has come to consider killing himself, he sketches a social situation that would fit almost any historical era:

> To whom can I speak today? One's fellows are evil; the friends of today do not love. To whom can I speak today? Faces have disappeared: Every man has a downcast face toward his fellow. To whom can I speak today? A man should arouse wrath by his evil character, but he stirs everyone to laughter, in spite of the wickedness of his sin. To whom can I speak today? There are no righteous; the land is left to those who do wrong. To whom can I speak today? The sin that afflicts the land, it has no end.[6]

Do evidences such as these mean that human nature is essentially wicked? Christians have somewhat blurred their response to this question. On the whole, Eastern Orthodox and Roman Catholics have tended to say no. For them, human beings, like the rest of creation, have been made good, and sin has not ravaged the core of human integrity. The cumulative effect of human wrongdoing has darkened people's minds and weakened people's wills, but the grace of God, the inner sharing that God offers, can heal these afflictions, restore reason and will to good health. On the whole, Protestants have come closer to saying yes. Both Luther and Calvin considered human nature deeply diseased, corrupt and pitted by sin. Only the sheer grace of God covered over this corruption, leaving human beings absolutely nothing of which to boast. We never have any merits before God. We must depend utterly on the divine mercy. So long as Christ hangs from the cross in our churches we shall have to suspect ourselves of fleeing the light because our deeds are evil.

An ecumenical, consensual reading of the Christian tradition would balance suspicion with hope. The historical record is such that we have always had good reason to look hard at human beings' motivations. That remains eminently true today. The lightest scratch at the surface of our military, industrial, educational, or ecclesiastical establishments reveals a sobering amount of self-service. In the areas of armaments, energy production, tax policy, entertainment, and health care (to take merely a sampling), waste and greed splatter the map. Realistically, human history is a very flawed story, pillage and war almost predominating.[7] We would be foolish indeed to conceive reality as though our tribe had not mightily resisted God's grace.

On the other hand, we would be more foolish not to configure reality around the places where our tribe has accepted God's grace and a thousand flowers have bloomed. In its art, invention, healing, education, parenting, science, and liturgy, the human species has proved God wise to have created, justified the angels of God for shouting with joy. The light still shines in the darkness. Most minds still feel the lure of truth. Given half a chance by their social circumstances, a majority of people still want to do what is right. Therefore we cannot accept the cynic's view that human sloth or venality usually will prevail. Every generation a few saints say things always might go better.

TWO

A Buddhist View

FOR WHAT ARE HUMAN BEINGS SEARCHING?

Buddhism began in the first part of the fifth century B.C.E. when an Indian prince named Gautama proclaimed a persuasive solution to the problem of human suffering. Known as the Buddha ("Enlightened One"), Gautama assumed that human beings were searching for an answer to the question of suffering (pain, confusion, dissatisfaction). The success of the Buddha's teaching (*Dharma*) over twenty-five hundred years suggests that this assumption was on the mark. Before the time of the Buddha, Indians had been concentrating on sacrifice. Led by priests who had become experts in intricate rituals, many Indians thought that sacrificing animals or grain or butter to one or more of the gods would make them harmonious with the cosmos and therefore prosperous. The Buddha, the Mahavira (the founder of Jainism, another significant Indian religion), and some of the sages who wrote the Upanishads, all were active around 500 B.C.E. opposing this sacrificial outlook. In their experience it did not work.

The Buddha, the Mahavira, and most of the Upanishadic sages agreed that a better way lay within. Where the priests stressed outward ritual actions, these leaders of the opposition stressed inner meditation. The sort of peace for which human beings are searching, they said, best comes from calming the body and the mind. So calmed, the person can start to analyze what flows down the stream of consciousness and realize that most of what we are depends upon how we think. As the *Dhammapada,* a much beloved little classic of Buddhist spirituality, put it somewhat later:

25

What we are today comes from our thoughts of yesterday, and our present thoughts build our life of tomorrow: our life is the creation of our mind. If a man speaks or acts with an impure mind, suffering follows him as the wheel of the cart follows the beast that draws the cart. What we are today comes from our thoughts of yesterday, and our present thoughts build our life of tomorrow: our life is the creation of our mind. If a man speaks or acts with a pure mind, joy follows him as his own shadow.[1]

Buddhism quickly developed a philosophical explanation of all of reality, and a full ethical code, but close to its heart has always lain the Buddha's original stress on meditation. Wisdom (philosophy), morality (ethics), and meditation have formed a sort of tripod, each leg reinforcing the others, but the whole structure would have collapsed without the insight, the vision, that the Buddha gained by sitting in meditation under the Bo tree (as Buddhist legend pictures him). It was when he vowed not to leave where he sat until he had solved the problem of suffering, and then ascended to the highest levels of meditation, that the Buddha accomplished the decisive deed, the victory that made him the Enlightened One.

As we shall see in the next section, the Buddha's own example has furnished his followers with much of their understanding of suffering, enlightenment, and liberation. Before turning to that example, however, let us make sure that we have this matter of seeking a solution to the problem of suffering securely in hand. It is a perennial matter, quite parallel to the Christian grapplings with sin. In every human life there is enough pain, confusion, or dissatisfaction to prod the individual to question where he is going, how she is living, what sense the whole human mess might make. By the time of the Buddha India had developed a tradition of pondering such religious questions. The deeper parts of the Vedas (the writings that became the Hindu scriptures) had invited the reader to ponder the origin of the world, and the early Upanishads had turned such pondering in the direction of the self. It is significant—a testimony to the equality of all human beings, whatever the age in which they live—that these ponderings can still grip our minds today.

The reason that the deeper parts of the Vedas, the early Upanishads, and the speeches of the Buddha can still grip our minds today is that we still suffer. Our lives are painful, spiritually if not materially. If we are fortunate enough not to have to worry about food and shelter, we still fret over the education of our children, or the failing health of our parents, or other emotional tensions. Local, national, and international politics give us a great deal to ponder soberly, and often our souls mirror the outer political chaos. Churches, psychiatrists, and a dozen faddish movements depend on our inner turmoil. Were peace of soul widespread and easy to obtain, many teachers, counselors, and writers would be out of business. But peace of soul, inner order, is not easy to obtain, as our statistics on mental illness, suicide, divorce, alcoholism, and drug abuse shout from the headlines. Twitching and turning, pursuing and fleeing, we are like a mass of lemmings trying to find a permanent outlet to the overcrowding of our souls.

"All life is suffering," the first of the Buddha's Four Noble Truths proclaims. All human beings find themselves in painful, imperfect situations. The difference between those who are wise and those who are foolish is that the wise stop distracting themselves long enough to face their situation and see its basic proportions. The beginning of a cure to one's sickness is the step of courage that takes one to the doctor, the spiritual physician who has solved the problem of suffering and knows the way to a solid peace.

OF WHAT USE IS THE BUDDHA?

The Buddha has served his followers, and the rest of the world, as a spiritual physician. His biography has exemplified how one can pass from a deep immersion in suffering to a sense of liberation and peace; his teaching laid out a straight path, so that others might come to a similar liberation and peace.

The key moment in the Buddha's biography was the time that Buddhists sometimes refer to as "the awakening." Born the son of a king, Gautama grew up sheltered from all unpleasant things. One day, however, he chanced to see an old man, and so began to ponder the threat of aging. Another day he saw a person who was diseased, and so began to contend with sickness. A third day he met a corpse, and so began to face human mortality. In the *Buddhacarita*, an account of the Buddha's life by the poet Ashvaghosa (first century C.E.), the young prince expressed his awakened awareness of death in the following words:

> This is the end which has been fixed for all, and yet the world forgets its fears and takes no heed! The hearts of men are surely hardened to fears, for they feel quite at ease even while traveling along the road to the next life. Turn back the chariot! [he had been out riding] This is no time or place for pleasure excursions. How could an intelligent person pay no heed at a time of disaster, when he knows of his impending destruction?[2]

The prince resolved to pay full heed, devoting all his energy to finding a way around the impasses of the human situation. He left the palace (where he had a wife and child), sought the advice of various holy men, and when their different regimes of austerities and meditations did not bring him liberation, sat himself under the Bo tree and vowed not to leave until he had solved his problem. In the course of his meditation he realized that the key to suffering is desire. We suffer because we want things, have attachments. If we would detach ourselves, extinguish our desires, we would give suffering no holds by which to grab us.

The Buddha emerged from his meditation convinced that he now had the key to a happy life. Polished and put into didactic form, his key became the Four Noble Truths: (1) All life is suffering. (2) The cause of suffering is desire. (3) Stopping desire will stop suffering. (4) One can stop desire by following the eightfold path of right views, right intention, right speech, right action, right livelihood, right effort, right mindfulness, and right concentration.

Right views and right intention comprise the wisdom portion of the Buddha's program: how we should think about reality. Right speech, action, and livelihood comprise the ethical portion: how we should behave. Right effort, mindfulness, and concentration comprise the meditational portion: how we should compose ourselves by inner *yoga*. Although these formulations are rather abstract, Buddhist commentators soon applied them to many concrete situations, putting together a full-bodied regime for stopping desire, ending suffering, and gaining full freedom.

After his enlightenment, the Buddha wandered from town to town, preaching the Four Noble Truths and other catechetical expressions of his insight. Thus in his famous Fire Sermon he portrayed the unliberated or unenlightened life as ablaze with desire: "All things, O priests, are on fire ... And with what are these on fire? With the fire of passion, say I, with the fire of hatred, with the fire of infatuation; with birth, old age, death, sorrow, lamentation, misery, grief, and despair are they on fire."[3]

The intent of the Buddha's preaching was to help people extinguish this fire. If he succeeded, people would escape what Indians called *samsara,* the basically painful situation in which they were fated to keep going endlessly around a circle of deaths and rebirths. If they could break this vicious circle, by extinguishing their desire, they would enter a state called *nirvana.* Buddhists have sometimes described nirvana as the state of the flame when the candle has been blown out. More positively, they have described nirvana as a state of unconditioned perfection—the freedom that comes when all ties are broken, all conditions removed.

The Buddha convinced his first followers that his teaching was true by personally manifesting the freedom he claimed his teaching could bring. His serenity, kindness, and depth won him thousands of disciples. These disciples formed a Buddhist community, called the *Sangha,* that offered a supportive social context for pursuing liberation from samsara, fulfillment in nirvana. Whether as celibates or laypeople, followers formally "took refuge" in the Buddha, the Dharma, and the Sangha, and so became members of the Enlightened One's family. They were taught a "middle way" between excessive austerity and self-indulgence, and as time passed they developed a rich Buddhist style in philosophy, art, and social relationships.

The more conservatively inclined followers, who today are represented by the Theravadin branch of the Buddhist family influential in Sri Lanka, Burma, and Thailand, continued to look upon the Buddha as essentially a man, a wise teacher and exemplar of the way to enlightenment. The Mahayanists, who have dominated East Asia, speculated that the Buddha embodied the essence of reality, the enlightenment being that we all possess, so they downplayed his humanity and emphasized his heavenly or symbolic aspects. Either way, all Buddhists looked back to Gautama as the one whose Noble Truths had launched their voyage.

HOW MAY WE HOPE TO GROW?

What sort of progress can a person who joins the Sangha hope to achieve? There are several ways that the Buddhist tradition has answered this question. First, any person who labors to be a faithful Buddhist, keeping the moral precepts, studying the wisdom literature, and meditating regularly can expect to improve his or her karmic condition. *Karma* is the law of cause and effect that rules the domain of samsara. At any given time, our state, the quality of our existence, reflects the merits or demerits we have accumulated in past lives. The most advantageous state is to be a human being (rather than an animal or even a god), because humans have the greatest chance to gain merit. Indeed, it is always possible for human beings to strive so mightily that they gain enlightenment, as the Buddha did. Even if full enlightenment does not come, however, the faithful Buddhist can hope to be born in more advantageous circumstances in the next life. Minimally, then, the faithful Buddhist may hope to grow closer to the condition from which eventually she or he will progress to enlightenment and nirvana.

Second, if we take a more interior look at a devout Buddhist's progress, we find an enhanced relationship to nature, other people, and the Buddhist's own self. As his will, mind, and heart are purified, the Buddhist starts to sense the meaning of the canonical teachings that reality is not plural. This lessens the separation that unenlightened people and cultures tend to make between the human being and nature, or among different human beings. The sense that separateness is an illusion grows in tandem with one's understanding of the Buddha's doctrine of *conditioned co-*

production. This doctrine pictures all reality as a chain of mutual influences, such that all aspects of consciousness and being are intimately linked. The result is the view that reality is a series of dynamic relationships, a fluid network or ecology in which nothing stands isolated.

As the person's development gets into high gear, it penetrates the difficult Buddhist conviction that the very notion of a separate human "self" is an illusion. According to Buddhist psychology, there is no *atman* or core identity to the human entity. Rather we are but temporary "heaps" of five component qualities (*skandhas*) and so have no substance or self to which to cling. The profound Buddhist philosophers have sensed that the last object of desire, the attachment to which we cling with greatest tenacity, is our own selfhood. To give up the "I" that has been the central referent of all our experience since childhood is an almost heroic act of detachment. So Buddhists stress the constant change that swirls both around us and inside us. Reality is not so much a stately series of clearly delineated beings as a smooth stream of constant alterations. As a person comes closer to enlightenment, she becomes better coordinated to this stream. She seems to grow better at hearing the deep music at the stream's depths and to become a more graceful dancer.

At this point, the traditional Buddhist description of reality as having "three marks" takes on a pregnant significance. According to mainstream Buddhist doctrine, we can characterize all reality as painful, fleeting, and having no substance or personal core. The first mark, pain, applies the first Noble Truth ("all life is painful") to each individual reality. Human beings always find, both in their own beings and in their circumstances, suffering, imperfection, confusion, mortality, and the like. The second mark, fleeting, applies to all individual existents, the flux, change, and relativity that we discussed above. Nothing in the world is static or permanent. Everything develops, waxes or wanes.

The third mark, having no substance or personal core (*an*atman), takes flux into the very heart of each being, including the human being. From the perspective of the Buddha's enlightened insight, all things are "empty." Nothing is full, solid, independent of the withering tides of samsara. As the *Heart Sutra,* a famous Mahayana text, puts it: "Avalokita, the Holy Lord and Bodhisattva, was moving in the deep course of the Wisdom which has gone beyond. He looked down from on high, He beheld but five heaps, and he saw that in their own-being they were empty."[4]

Avalokita is a famous Buddhist saint or *bodhisattva* (one who has come to the verge of enlightenment and nirvana). Having entered deeply into the wisdom of enlightenment *(prajnaparamita),* which goes beyond ordinary, unenlightened thinking, he saw no independent beings, only clusters of skandhas. They had no self or substance. In their inmost being they were empty.

The sutra goes on to show that emptiness characterizes all of samsaric reality. If we are wise, therefore, we will cling to nothing in the world of space and time. Nothing in the world of space and time is permanent. Everything is bound to disappoint us and cause us sorrow. The more enlightened we become, the more detached we become from everything samsaric. In this lies our freedom. At the limit, we come to the ecstatic realization that even we ourselves have no own-being, are empty. As a Japanese businessman expressed it in the euphoria of *satori* or enlightenment: "I've totally disappeared. Buddha is!"[5]

WHAT DO WE OWE ONE ANOTHER?

Like all religious traditions, the Buddhist maintains that we first owe one another a consistency between our thinking and our doing. If we are committed to Buddhist doctrine, we owe other people a behavior honestly in keeping with Buddhist doctrine. Thus we owe other people detachment from desire, brisk progress along the Eightfold Path, resolute efforts to come to enlightenment and nirvana. If we are professing to be Buddhists, people should find our ideas, words, and deeds ringing true to Buddhist ideals.

Second, we owe one another a great compassion. This virtue and emotion *(mahakaruna)* is an overflow of the Buddhist view that all life is painful. One who takes the first Noble Truth seriously should be moved to pity for all living things, since all living things inevitably are suffering. As the notion of the three marks shows, it is the very marrow of samsaric, conditioned existence to be painful, fleeting, and substanceless. Minimally, the person who believes this should strive not to increase other creatures' sufferings. More generously, he may decide to take the bodhisattva vow, which is to labor for the enlightenment and liberation of all living things (if need be, postponing his own nirvana). If Buddhist wisdom stresses the interrelatedness of all creation, Buddhist mahakaruna stresses our common fate. In place of conflict and violence, it urges peace and mutual support. In place of ego and competition, it urges selflessness and cooperation.

Third, Buddhist ethicians have developed a refined moral code *(sila)* that has set before the Buddhist laity five major precepts, under the assumption that the generous observance of these precepts would greatly enhance human beings' commonweal. The first precept is to refrain from killing living creatures. The second is to refrain from stealing. The third forbids sexual impurity. The fourth forbids lying. The fifth forbids drinking alcoholic beverages. Monks have had a more detailed moral code, suited to their close living together in community, but the five basic precepts have been the ethical foundation of monks' social lives as well.

In his influential little book *Small Is Beautiful*, the British economist E. F. Schumacher spoke of a "Buddhist Economics" that he had glimpsed while working in Burma as a consultant. Schumacher's decription captures the spirit of what Buddhists, at their best, have felt they owed one another in the central area of work: "The Buddhist point of view takes the function of work to be at least threefold: to give a man a chance to utilise and develop his faculties; to enable him to overcome his ego-centredness by joining with other people in the common task; and to bring forth the goods and services needed for a becoming existence."[6]

As Schumacher further notes, the good consequences that might flow from this view of work are endless. For example, it would mean that organizing work so that it became boring, meaningless, stultifying, or nerve-wracking would be criminal. Similarly, to be more concerned with goods than with people, with products than with workers, would be a great evil: a terrible lack of compassion, a strong attachment to material goods. Last, to flee from work and long for leisure would be to misunderstand both the humanizing nature of work and the complementarity of work and leisure, which ought to be like the beat and rest of our pulses.

Central to Buddhists' sociology, therefore, is a degree of detachment or nonstriving that the West usually finds difficult to understand. The things that properly bind people together are interior, not exterior. The true goods we ought to be pursuing are states of soul, not numbers in bank books. Buddhist culture has always realized that people must have certain material necessities. Good food, shelter, clothing, health care, and the like have never been denigrated. But the Buddhist ideal has been for these material necessities to serve people's progress in deeper matters, such as detachment and mutual compassion.

Thus, in the matter of clothing, Schumacher characterizes the Buddhist outlook as follows:

> If the purpose of clothing is a certain amount of temperature comfort and an attractive appearance, the task is to attain this purpose with the smallest possible effort, that is, with the smallest annual destruction of cloth and with the help of designs that involve the smallest possible input of toil. The less toil there is, the more time and strength is left for artistic creativity. It would be highly uneconomic, for instance, to go in for complicated tailoring, like the modern West, when a much more beautiful effect can be achieved by the skillful draping of uncut material. It would be the height of folly to make material so that it should wear out quickly and the height of barbarity to make anything ugly, shabby or mean.[7]

So, inspiringly enough, Buddhist economics turns out to have a central place for beauty. High among the things we owe one another are clean material surroundings, refined human manners, art and literature that please the soul. One can see these Buddhist ideals realized in the best of East Asian culture: Chinese landscape painting, Japanese shrine gardens, the refined etiquette idealized throughout the East. The famous Zen Rock Garden of Kyoto, for example, has translated the doctrine of emptiness into a spiritual refreshment and delight for millions of visitors.

HOW SHOULD WE CONCEIVE REALITY?

For Buddhists, reality is perhaps lighter and more fluent than it has been for most Western religionists. Buddhists can be utterly serious about striving for enlightenment, and remarkably disciplined, but their view of the world leaves considerable room for play. By play we do not mean frivolity or mindless fun. Rather we mean an artful style, a spontaneity, a light touch that keeps things from becoming grim and burdensome. At any given moment, the devoted Buddhist wants to be doing what he should be doing. Without divisions or distractions, she wants to give herself totally to the work, study, conversation, or recreation that is at hand. But the ideal mode of this immersion in what is real here and now is not harried or pressured. It is composed, self-contained, peaceful. The cycles of transmigration give Buddhists a large time frame in which to set the business of attaining nirvana. The doctrines of detachment and emptiness pry their fingers away from either materialist or intellectualist fixations. For those with eyes to see, a simple garden or a flower can convey all of creation's intrinsic perfection. The more enlightened one becomes, the more what is is satisfying.

Thus Buddhism says that we should conceive reality as in good measure a function of our own degree of enlightenment. If reality seems multiple, conflicted, oppressive, the fault is largely with our own perceptions. In itself, for the truly wise, reality is unified, harmonious, welcoming. As our ethical improvement, study, and meditation improve our perceptions, samsara starts to move toward nirvana. We find emptiness increasing and it starts to free us up to enjoy a more mobile reality, an invitation to dance. In some of the most advanced Buddhist schools of philosophy, samsara and nirvana are seen to be one. Nirvana is in the midst of samsara. To find perfection right here and now, one need only break the veils of illusion, see the here and now as it really is in its own-being.

The Vajrayana Buddhists, who represent the third major tradition (Theravada, Mahayana, Vajrayana), have placed special emphasis on the union of nirvana and samsara. Using mandalas (magical figures), mantras (magical sounds), and highly imaginative rituals, they have urged disciples to undercut the discursive, either-or sort of thinking that dominates the unenlightened and unite themselves on all levels with a reality that is unified. Marshaling emotional and psychic forces, the Vajrayanists have helped their adherents *feel* as well as think their way through the labyrinth of samsara, develop the emotional resonances that disclose nirvana's presence in the midst of the here and now.

Vajrayana has perhaps exerted its greatest influence in Tibet, and Tibetan Buddhist lore has featured some wonderful holy men whose eccentricities and austerities dramatize the assault on ordinary, unenlightened thinking that Vajrayana sometimes encourages. Tilopa is one of these holy men, a renowned saint and the teacher (guru) of the equally famous holy man Naropa. From the legends of Naropa's initiation by Tilopa comes the following story:

> Tilopa again sat motionless and silent for a year. Naropa made the appropriate gesture, circumambulated him with folded hands, spoke his prayers and, when once Tilopa glanced at him, asked for instruction. "If you want the Dharma, follow me," said Tilopa and went away. When they met a minister conducting his bride home on an elephant, Tilopa said: "If I had had a disciple he would have pulled them down and dragged them about." Naropa did so, but the minister and his attendants beat Naropa thoroughly and when he was unable to move with pain Tilopa came and asked: "Naropa, what is wrong with you?" Naropa answered: "You cannot play with this craftsman of a minister, in a jest he ground me to a powder, and so I suffer." Tilopa said: "This rock of your body believing in an I must be ground to powder, Naropa. Look into the mirror of your mind, the radiant light, the mysterious home of the Dakini." When he had healed him with his hand he gave him the instruction on the radiant light, the inexistence of the darkness of unknowing.[8]

Naropa's gestures around Tilopa conjure the ceremonial atmosphere of many Vajrayana exercises. Tilopa is like a silent mountain of wisdom, and Naropa can only gain access to this wisdom by becoming emotionally attuned to its otherworldly style. Tilopa stresses that the teaching demands sacrifice, even suffering. The beating that Naropa receives is meant to prepare his mind for the insight that there is no "I." What the minister and his attendants have done to Naropa Naropa must do to his illusions and attachments. Tilopa wants him to come to see that his mind is filled with light. *It* is the real home of all godly forces like the Dakini (imps attending the Hindu goddess Kali). The mind is a radiant light, a knowledge *(bodhi)* being. The darkness of ignorance is an illusion. Reality itself is pure blazing light.

Not all Buddhists have pictured reality so vividly, but all orthodox Buddhists have finally depended upon the the Master's conviction that when we extinguish desire we behold a reality unmarred by suffering, untainted by ignorance. Within each of us, the Buddhist saints have taught, a perfection is waiting to blaze forth. This perfection is more real than our divisions and errors, more ultimate and important.

THREE

A Hindu View

FOR WHAT ARE HUMAN BEINGS SEARCHING?

"Hinduism" is a broad term, a sort of umbrella for many of the religious movements that have arisen on the Indian subcontinent since the interaction of native peoples (Dravidians) with invaders from the Northwest (Aryans) that began about four thousand years ago. The Aryan invaders were a nomadic bunch of warriors whose oral literature formed the basis of most of the *Vedas,* the Hindu scriptures. The people who have honored the Vedas as the highest source of wisdom have been welcome to stand under the umbrella called "Hinduism." The people (such as the Buddhists and Jains) who have not honored the Vedas as their highest religious authority have stood outside the umbrella. In terms of our first question, the initial Hindu response probably would be that human beings are searching for the saving light that dawned in the minds of the seers *(rishis)* whose visions were the core inspiration of the Vedas.

As Hinduism sees it, the problem standing between human beings and happiness is ignorance. Wash away ignorance with knowledge and you have opened the way to happiness. Still, both ignorance and knowledge have carried different overtones with different Hindu groups. For the priestly tradition represented in the Vedas, sacrifice was the key religious act. Through sacrifice a person became harmonious with the divine powers running the cosmos. Consequently, the most injurious ignorance was not knowing the forms and meanings of the sacrifices, while the most valuable knowledge was knowing the words, actions, gestures and the like that went into an efficacious ritual. At its extreme, this priestly tradition (called Brahminism) held that the sacrifical words had an unfailing efficacy. Pronounce them correctly and the good effects of the sacrifice were bound to follow.

In opposition to such a magical outlook, other people reflecting on the Vedic tradition turned away from sacrifice and ritual. For the schools represented in the Upanishads, the poetico-philosophical musings one finds at the end of the Vedic corpus, the worst ignorance was not verbal and ritualistic but interior. Not to know the self and the ultimate ground of reality was what caused human beings' unhappiness. Conversely, to grasp the true nature of the self and see its union with Brahman, the ground of all reality, opened the gates to happiness and freedom. Consequently, the Upanishadic seers stressed interior exercises of thought and quiet mind-control. They were *yogins,* people disciplined to control the many levels of human consciousness. Where the earlier Vedists and priests had tended to concentrate on a plurality of gods, most of whom personified natural forces like fire or the storm, the Upanishadic yogins sought something simpler. The self *(atman)* and the ultimate ground of all creation (Brahman) both seemed to the Upanishadic seers rather impersonal. The quiet core lying underneath all sensations, feelings, images, and discursive (step by step) thinking intrigued the yogins. Their interest was pure consciousness, intelligibility, and being.

The Isa Upanishad, one of the shortest, expresses some of the themes typical of the Upanishads overall: "The Self is one. Unmoving it moves swifter than thought. The senses do not overtake it, for always it goes before. Remaining still, it outstrips all that run. Without the Self, there is no life. To the ignorant the Self appears to move—yet it moves not. From the ignorant it is far distant—yet it is near. It is within all, and it is without all."[1]

For the Isa, the atman is a unity and a paradox. At the center or base of any of us, it seems not to move, yet to be the explanation for movement quick as thought. It is ahead of the senses, and ahead of everything else that moves. It is that nodal mystery, the still point of the racing world. Ignorant people think that it changes and alters, but it does not. It is poles apart from the conceptions of the unwise, yet their inmost point of identity. The self, in fact, is that limit reality that falls outside such disjunctions as "within" and "without." Those disjunctions come from something subsequent to the self: our minds that work piecemeal, separating and distinguishing. The atman is prior, more primordial, the mysterious beginning we must grasp if we are to gain the light that can make us free.

Later Hindu philosophers such as Shankara (ca. 788–820) tried to systematize the basic intuitions of the Upanishads, laying great stress on the oneness of atman and Brahman. Other Hindus found these meditations too difficult or abstract, and so gave themselves over to more devotional religious practices, stressing love of such gods as Krishna and Shiva. This love *(bhakti)* inevitably bolstered the personal side of Hindu ultimate reality. Where the Upanishadic seers and later philosophers stressed the impersonal side, the bhaktas pictured Krishna and Shiva on the order of human beings, able to know, will, and feel. Indeed, the *Bhagavad-Gita,* Hinduism's most popular writing, offers as its highest revelation the assurance of Krishna that he himself loves human beings. For the *Gita,* therefore, human beings are searching for a knowledge that is "interpersonal," shot through with love and affection.

OF WHAT USE IS REVELATION?

Hinduism has no single figure, such as Jesus or Gautama, who functions as its prime authority and exemplar of religious truth. Hindus sometimes worship Krishna parallel to the way that Christians worship Jesus, but in the main scholars regard Krishna not as a historical person but as an *avatar* (symbolic manifestation) of Vishnu, one of the three major gods that comprise the Hindu trinity (Brahma, Vishnu, Shiva). So it is the Vedas that serve as the central Hindu authority, and the Vedas spotlight the phenomenon of revelation. The insights of the seers from whom the Vedas are thought to have derived were flashes of light in which ultimate reality disclosed its inmost nature. By appropriating the wisdom of the Vedas, and the rest of the orthodox tradition, Hindus can repeat the experiences of the original seers. Especially in meditation, they too can be flooded by the revelatory light of ultimate reality.

Through its long history Hinduism has pondered Vedic wisdom from every angle, and several principal spiritual paths have emerged. Since different people have different religious inclinations and needs, there should be a catholic variety of ways. Indeed, the *Bhagavad-Gita* owes much of its popularity to the fact that it offers several different ways to reach *moksha* or ultimate freedom. Like the Christian New Testament, its teaching is not uniform but pluralistic.

For example, the Gita approves the traditional yogas of meditation and philosophical study, repeating the long-held Hindu belief that both calming the senses and the spirit, so that one can enter the deep stillness of *samadhi* (thoughtless trance), and bringing the mind to an intuitive grasp of reality, can spring the person free from samsara. As much as Buddhism, but with some variation, Hinduism thinks in terms of reincarnation. Until a person has broken free of the cycles of dying and being reborn, she or he is condemned to much suffering. The yogas of meditation and philosophical study both aim at freeing the atman from the bonds of samsara.

They are not exercises of relaxation or academic learning but religious efforts to gain ultimate freedom.

The Gita is more famous, however, for having offered two other yogas. *Karma-yoga* stems from the notion that one need not flee the world and refrain from action, but that action itself can be a liberating discipline, so long as one acts desirelessly, without clinging to the fruits of one's labors. If a person can remain unperturbed, neither depressed in time of failure nor exalted in time of success, then action can grind away his bad karma, preparing him for moksha and deep freedom. Mahatma Gandhi, India's liberator from British colonial rule, was a strong advocate of karma-yoga. One of Gandhi's favorite illustrations of acting without regard to the action's outcome was working at a spinning wheel. The person who worked her wheel peacefully, joining her spirit to its endless revolutions and not caring overmuch about the quantity of her production, could lessen her bad karma and emerge from her work considerably purified.

Bhakti-yoga, the Gita's fourth path, is a discipline of love. The disciple who choses this path probably is somewhat emotional, and bhakti-yoga's trick is to convert this emotion into useful religious energy. If a person falls in love with Krishna or Shiva, praying ardently at the god's shrines and resolving to purify his life so as to be worthy of the god's corresponding love, he may make great religious progress. Love has an inclination toward generosity and self-denial. Among ardent Hindu bhaktas it often leads to fasts and austerities, as well as to lyrical poetry. Indeed, the masses of ordinary Indians probably have found bhakti-yoga the most attractive of Hinduism's several paths. They may not be able to meditate and attain samadhi, but they can feel and love enthusiastically.

Krishna's final disclosures in the Gita stress the high value of religious love and illustrate well the impact of Hindu revelation: "Listen again to my highest work, the most secret of all. You are loved by me surely, and I will tell you for your good. Set your mind on me, belong to me, worship me and bow before me. You shall come to me alone. Truly I promise you. You are dear to me. Forsaking all things of the law, come to me as your single shelter. Do not be sad, I will save you from all evil."[2]

The value of such revelation, in any religious tradition, is that it seems to come with divine authority. Where the words of human beings are varied and suspect, we can cling with complete trust to the voice that seems to come from heaven. Today our sophistication about textual interpretation and depth psychology makes us leery of "revelations," but through most of humankind's history special disclosures by God have been accepted almost as a matter of course. They were always fraught with awe, but ancient people expected the divine to manifest itself in such natural prodigies as earthquakes, such human experiences as a striking dream. Hindu divinity, like the divinity of most other peoples, has been expressive, manifestive. Continually it has disclosed its light, love, and life. For Hindus, the Vedas have centered a stream of divine revelation that yogins, *sages,* self-less workers, and ardent *bhaktas* all might feel flowing within them. Consistently, the revelatory message has been to orient one's life toward more ultimate things: the self that grounds one's personal existence, the love of the God who proclaims that divinity itself is loving.

HOW MAY WE HOPE TO GROW?

If we follow the religious traditions derived from Hindu revelation, we may hope to grow freer and freer of samsaric bondage. One of the most interesting ways that Hinduism schematized such growth was in terms of four life-cycle stages. The scheme probably was more an ideal than a schedule which the majority of people strove practically to meet, but it laid before the upper castes, who were thought to have a good chance to obtain moksha in their present life, an influential sketch of how ideally they might develop. (In addition, it has intrigued such Western analysts of the life-cycle as Erik Erikson, whose study of Gandhi was motivated in good part by his desire to observe a prime specimen of middle aged "generativity" [Erikson's term for the productiveness that maturity should bring] who had been rooted in a non-European culture.)[3]

The first stage in the classical Hindu scheme was studenthood. The young boy (girls may have received a full religious education in early Vedic times, but by the time of the classical law codes—around 100 C.E. —they married early and received only an abridged education) began his training by going to live with a guru and studying the Vedas. Through this period of religious instruction, he was to learn the sacred texts by heart, preserve full chastity, and be completely obedient to his teacher. The hope was that a deep immersion in the sacred tradition would so form the boy's mind and character that later he would have at his fingertips the knowledge which greater experience could transmute into wisdom.

When he had reached his early twenties, the young man was expected to complete his education, return to social life at large, marry, and assume family responsibilities. Hindus usually have lived in extended families, with three generations interacting vigorously, and usually they have placed great stress on generating children, especially males. (Parents have thought that they needed male children for their support in old age, and to perform the religious rituals necesary for the parents' successful journey to the next life.) Thus procreation has been more important than the emotional fulfillment of the spouses, and parents have arranged most marriages, through complicated transactions focusing on the size of the bride's dowry, the social status of the prospective spouses' families, the temperamental harmony of the prospective spouses, and so forth.

Both marriage and business have had a respectable status in Hindu culture, if only because the religious philosophers realized that most people were going to be married and engaged in commerce or agriculture. Of the four legitimate life-aims that Hindu culture admitted (pleasure, wealth, duty, and liberation), the first three usually were pursued in the married state. Pleasure *(kama)* included sexual satisfaction, good food, art, sports, and aesthetic enjoyments. Wealth *(artha)* entailed social responsibilities, and could be a religious hindrance, but in itself was nothing evil. Duty *(dharma)* will occupy us considerably in the next section, but here we can note that the householder had a clear place in society and, if he fulfilled what was generally expected of him, could hold his head high.[4]

The third life-stage came into view when a man realized that his hair had grown gray and he was gazing upon his children's children. These were to be signs to him that it was time to raise his sights to the fourth and highest of the Hindu life-aims, *moksha*. Progressively, he should withdraw from secular affairs, family matters as well as business, and betake himself from the town to the forest. In the forest (whether actual woods or some other secluded retreat) he was mainly to meditate, trying to apply several decades of worldly experience to the traditional teaching he had received as a boy. That teaching had laid out the ideal of detachment, the explanation of reincarnation, the duties of social life, and the techniques of meditation that the tradition said had been handed down by wise forebears. Such wisdom could mean little to a young person without much experience of love, work, politics, or the other major forces that constitute the way of the world. As a forest-dweller, the Hindu in the third state of his life was to make his personal experience and his tradition's ideals confront one another, under the expectation that now the light of revelation might shine deep into his own soul, illumining the real significance of what he had experienced as a householder.

The fourth and consummating phase of the idealized Hindu life-cycle portrayed the aged man, now standing in the sight of death, as a wandering holy man *(sannyasin)*. If his meditations in the forest had borne full fruit, he would have come to moksha, enlightenment and liberation, and moksha would have completely detached him from worldly desires. Wandering in the simplest of clothing, begging his food and experiencing the presence of the divine everywhere, the perfected Hindu could show others the freedom the tradition had always promised was possible. Mainly through his example, but also through his explanations and good counsel, he could keep alive in Hindu society what revelation actually meant. For, fine as the traditional scriptures might be, people most needed to see living embodiments of the scriptural wisdom. The fourth stage of the life-cycle challenged all men to become such embodiments. (Women were counseled to wait until their next incarnation, when they might return as males.)

WHAT DO WE OWE ONE ANOTHER?

Through its social philosophers, such as the authors of the authoritative *Laws of Manu* (second century B.C.E. to second century C.E.), Hinduism laid down rather detailed prescriptions for what human beings owe one another. Essentially, we owe one another the faithful performance of the duties that fall to our particular social class. Since Vedic times Indian society has had a fivefold social stratification. At the top of society are the priests, next come the warriors, third come the merchants and farmers, fourth are the workers, and outside the acceptable classes stand the outcastes or untouchables. Each of these social levels had certain rights and duties, the happy functioning of which was encouraged by the notion of *dharma*. In Hinduism, as in Buddhism, dharma can mean teaching, but here it is the implication of "class responsibility" that should be stressed. In the *Bhagavad-Gita*, for example, Krishna tells Arjuna, a young warrior, that his objections to fighting cannot finally stand, since fighting is part of his class-responsibility. To throw off his class-responsibility, and behave as though he were a priest or a merchant, would be a disgrace: "Better to do your own task imperfectly than do another's well. Better die in your own duty; another's task brings peril." (3:35, Stanford trans.)

Law codes such as *Manu* specified the tasks of the different classes rather closely. For example, *Manu* sets before the priest six requisite acts: teaching, studying, sacrificing for himself, sacrificing for others, making gifts, and receiving gifts. The warrior class, led by the king, amounted to the secular power, the arm of the law empowered to enforce the priests' understanding of all the classes' dharma. The king was to protect his subjects, but also to expand his kingdom—by fair means or foul. The individual warrior had the responsibility of killing the enemy, or being killed by the enemy, and this violent aspect of his vocation set the *Mahabharata*, Hinduism's greatest epic, its central ethical dilemma: How could one reconcile the warrior's dharma with the religious ideal of *ahimsa* (nonviolence)? The Gita, which is part of the *Mahabharata*, balances Krishna's advice to Arjuna (fight!) with an explanation of the soul's immortality. In killing, a warrior only slays the body of his enemy, not the enemy's soul. Moreover, if he goes to war dispassionately, without attachment to victory or plunder, he may make this admittedly hard part of his class-dharma something salutary for his spiritual growth.

The merchant class, who probably were the majority, were supposed to concentrate on agriculture and trade. *Manu* indicates some of the merchant's main duties:

> [He] must know the respective value of gems, pearls, of coral, of metals, of (cloth) made of thread, of perfumes, and of condiments. He must be acquainted with the (manner of) sowing seeds, and of the good and bad qualities of fields, and he must perfectly know all measures and weights. Moreover, the excellence and defects of commodities, the advantages and disadvantages of (different) countries, the (probable) profit and loss on merchandise, and the means of properly rearing cattle.[5]

The worker class was much lower than the other three. Whereas priests, warriors, and merchants could receive the Hindu sacraments (e.g., the sacred thread that signified rebirth and candidacy for moksha), the workers (or slaves) were not considered twice-born and had no access to the Vedas. R. C. Zaehner summarizes their situation as follows:

> The Brahmans [priests] were and are the custodians of the Veda, and they should instruct the other two "twice-born" classes in Vedic lore, but on no account should instruction be given to a Sudra [worker], let alone an outcaste: that would be an appalling sin and is punished by the pains of hell. The Sudras, indeed, were regarded as being so impure that they were denied all access to the Veda, they might not sacrifice or have sacrifices offered on their behalf, nor might they associate with the twice-born. The Sudra was created a slave, and even if manumitted by his master, a slave he remains, for no merely human agency can alter the eternal *dharma* as interpreted by the Brahmans.[6]

The main responsibility of a worker, then, was to work—to be a silent, respectful, unenvious servant, hoping by this good behavior to merit a better rebirth.

The outcastes or untouchables fell outside the normal socioreligious order completely. None of the four castes could touch them without being defiled; they could not enter Hindu temples; they had to create their own priesthood; even their gods had no place in the Hindu pantheon. When Gandhi launched his campaign against British rule, by nonviolent protest and fasting, he also took on the Hindu institution of untouchability. Making himself the champion of the outcastes, whom he called the *Harijans* or "Children of God," he forced the Hindu conscience to admit that untouchability was deeply wrong and got the Hindu temples opened to the outcastes.

Hindu women of all classes generally had the status of wards. In childhood they were subject to their fathers, in maturity to their husbands, and in older age (widowhood) to their eldest son. Through much of Hindu history they were betrothed in childhood, married by puberty, honored mainly for bearing sons, expected always to be gentle and submissive, and encouraged to throw themselves on their husband's funeral pyre. *Manu* was sufficiently suspicious of women to counsel that a man should not sit alone even with his mother or his sister, and sometimes fathers announced the birth of a girl child with the dolorous line, "Nothing was born."

HOW SHOULD WE CONCEIVE REALITY?

Mircea Eliade, the Rumanian-born dean of American historians of religion, began his illustrious career by studying yoga in India. Early in his famous work *Yoga* Eliade suggests that Hindu reality has stood on four conceptual pillars:

> Four basic and interdependent concepts, four "kinetic ideas," bring us directly to the core of Indian spirituality. They are *karma, maya, nirvana,* and *yoga* . . . In terms of Western philosophy, we can say that, from the post-Vedic period on, India has above all sought to understand (1) the law of universal causality, which connects man with the cosmos and condemns him to transmigrate indefinitely. This is the law of *karma.* (2) The mysterious process that engenders and maintains the cosmos and, in so doing, makes possible the "eternal return" of existences. This is *maya,* cosmic illusion, endured (even worse-accorded validity) by man as long as he is blinded by ignorance *(avidya).* (3) Absolute reality, "situated" somewhere beyond the cosmic illusion woven by *maya* and beyond human experience as conditioned by *karma;* pure Being, the Absolute, by whatever name it may be called—the Self *(atman), brahman,* the unconditioned, the transcendent, the immortal, the indestructible, *nirvana,* etc. (4) The means of attaining to Being, the effectual techniques for gaining liberation. This corpus of means constitutes Yoga properly speaking.[7]

Karma and *maya* are closely linked, since karma is the "law" that obtains in the realm of maya. Maya is virtually a synonym for samsara: the realm of rebirth and suffering. However, the term maya lays more stress on the falsity of this realm, the ways in which it is a product of human ignorance or illusion. Maya also can connote a play, a sportive product of the creative powers, who conjure the nets of illusion like magicians.

To escape from maya one must move from ignorance to knowledge, as we have previously seen. The benefit of this move, the new territory to which it takes us is Being or *nirvana*. Whereas maya is becoming and fakery, nirvana is stable and utterly real. Buddhists have used the term nirvana to indicate the unconditioned state of fulfillment that enlightenment can bring. Hindus have spoken more of brahman and atman, the founding principle of the objective world and the corresponding foundation of the self. When Hindus have focused on the process of release, from maya into Being, they usually have used the word *moksha*.

We have seen some of the major yogas or disciplines by which Hindus have striven after moksha. All the yogas have assumed that one must labor mightily, gaining much self-control, if moksha is to become a strong possibility. The yoga that Eliade emphasizes, and that most Hindu holy men have gone into the forest to practice, is *dhyana* (meditation): controlling the senses, quieting the mind, and descending to the depths of pure consciousness. Patanjali (ca. 400 C.E.), the author of the classic text on this yoga, summarizes his subject matter as follows: "The eight limbs of yoga are: the various forms of abstention from evil-doing (yama), the various observances (niyamas), posture (asana), control of the prana [breath] (pranayama), withdrawal of the mind from sense objects (pratyahara), concentration (dharana), meditation (dhyana) and absorption in the atman (samadhi)."[8]

In the classical yogic regime, therefore, the first concerns are moral. One must reject evil-doing and start on the path of right-doing. Next come the disciplines of posture (sitting in what Buddhists call the lotus position, with one's spinal column erect) and breath control (unifying one's mind-body by regulating the intake and outflow of the breath). When these disciplines have been mastered, the more interior work can begin. The yogin withdraws his mind from sense objects, brings it to an objectless focus, and tries to develop a purer and purer consciousness (a simpler, more intense awareness, not focused on sensible objects or colored by discursive thoughts). The last stage of the yogin's journey takes him into *samadhi,* deep absorption in the spiritual principle that is the inmost reality of both the human self and the external world.

A description of the samadhi of Ma Jnanananda, a contemporary guru teaching in Madras, will perhaps make this state more intelligible (and also show that, on occasion, women have defied the normal social scheme and come to the highest religious authority). Ma ("Mother") Jnanananda reports that her trancelike states of absorption in ultimate reality began when she was a young girl:

> I knew that I was standing by a sea. At first there were others with me, then I was alone. The waves rose up, and I felt they would wash me away.

I was afraid, but later I fearlessly experienced complete immersion in the waves. In my early journeys into samadhi I sometimes saw the moon shining on a completely darkened ocean. This, the Shankaracharya [her guru] told me, is one of the signs of the true *jnani* [enlightened person]. I also experienced, and still experience, a blinding white light in this state.[9]

Overall, then, Hinduism tells us that we should conceive reality as bileveled. For lower, ordinary perception, reality is changing and pain-ridden, the realm of transmigration. For higher, extraordinary perception, reality is a blinding white light, a state of being-bliss-awareness. The ultimate charge that Hinduism lays on human beings, the opportunity it finally holds out, is to gain extraordinary perception, by some form of purifying yoga.

PART TWO

Evil

Almost all people engaged in the human quest stumble when they run into evil. Anticipating that their lives can be good, that they can find happiness for themselves and their loved ones, they run into nature's caprice or human malice and their hopes scatter like jacks. The result is a new, sobered outlook in which "reality" becomes morally ambiguous. As the introduction to a recent collection of essays on the problem of evil puts it: "We live in a morally ambiguous world. Most of us experience moments of contentment, happiness, even joy. But there is much unhappiness, discontent, and pain in the world as well. There is undeserved suffering, grinding poverty, excruciating pain, irrational acts of violence, and sudden sinister twists of fate."[1]

The writer of these sentences backed up his thesis with five items from just one day's worth of news *(The Los Angeles Times,* March 16, 1980): Two people in Indiana had been charged with reckless homicide in the death of a 74-year-old mentally retarded man whom they had kept as a slave. More than 21,000 barrels of oil spilled from a tanker was polluting forty miles of the Brittany coast. A man playing pool for 25 cents a game had become so enraged with his opponents that he shot one dead and wounded the other critically. Canine distemper in Monrovia, California, had led to the death of nine raccoons and a fear for the safety of all domestic animals. A "death ray" demonstration in New Mexico would soon test the possibility of destroying air-to-air missiles by laser.

Obviously these items vary in their degree of seriousness, and in the sort of evil they suggest. But each shows that our world always has only a thin shield against human or natural evils. At any given hour, a supposedly

47

rational person may knife one of his fellows for the price of a beer, a storm may kill dozens of people through flooding, a superpower is employing hundreds of scientists to develop weapons of nearly unimaginable destruction. These aspects of evil and threat are partly very new and partly as old as humanity itself. If it is new for human beings to have to worry about nuclear war or chemical pollution, it is very old for human beings to have to worry about fire, famine, and flood. From the beginning, life has been perilous. Thus Jean Auel's fine novel about the life of a paleolithic tribe, *The Clan of the Cave Bear,* begins with a vivid description of an earthquake along the Caspian Sea.[2] As archeological remains have verified, earthquakes were part of everyday life for the people of ancient Iran and Iraq, who have furnished us some of our most interesting data about prehistoric human existence. As long as there have been strange animals like us who can reflect, there has been worry about disease and death, fear of life's darkness and so gratitude for life's light.

In this Part we deal with Taoist, Buddhist, and Christian views of evil. Taoism has roots in prehistoric China, where *shamans* sought ecstatic union with the ultimate forces that ran the natural world. Out of these shamans' searches came both the Confucian and the Taoist interest in nature's Way (*Tao*). The Confucian interest was ethical: how to form the character of political leaders so that they could bring about good social life. The Taoist interest was poetic: how to make beautiful, free lives. Both Chinese groups felt that the best way to answer their questions was to listen to the cosmos.

For the Confucians, the great men of the past (Confucianism gave little power to women), the model rulers of old, had attuned themselves to nature by self-discipline, meditation, and graceful rituals. For the Taoists, union with the Way was interior and paradoxical. As the *Tao Te Ching,* Taoism's most honored text, puts it: "Those who know do not speak; those who speak do not know. Block the passages, shut the doors, let all sharpness be blunted, all tangles untied, all glare tempered."[3] Much of the reason we suffer is that we babble ignorantly, leave the doors of our soul open to the winds of distraction, strive for clarity in a world that never will be clear. Until we learn that nature treats us like the straw dogs used in the ritual sacrifices, we shall have false expectations and so suffer more than we might. Thus Lao Tzu, the reputed author of the *Tao Te Ching,* counseled unlearning our spontaneous expectations.

Buddhism and Christianity, as you no doubt suspect, have their own analyses of evil. For them the way around evil is the path of their founder, Gautama or Jesus. Gautama cut the heart out of evil by removing human desire. Jesus crushed Satan, evil's personification, by absorbing Satan's power into a more powerful divine love.

Nonetheless evil remains a deep mystery, a profound surd or irrational power. In contemplating the things that instinctively we feel should not be, all religious traditions have gotten down to their very bedrock. So in this Part we deal with some of humanity's most astringent symbols and reflections. Through history the Taoist, Buddhist, and Christian responses to evil have both formed the outlooks of billions of people and challenged some of humanity's very best minds. Insofar as evil shows no sign of vacating the human scene, the Taoist, Buddhist, and Christian responses continue to be relevant. Today, as in the past, many people find them to be lifesavers—buoys to cling to in the worst of storms.

FOUR

A Taoist View

HOW SHOULD WE VIEW NATURE?

Taoism has had two distinct historical phases, an early philosophical period, in which it gained most of its religious distinction, and a latter alchemical period, in which it had sizeable influence on the Chinese masses.[1] Through both periods, however, nature was a preoccupying interest. Our remarks will draw mainly from the works of Lao Tzu and Chuang Tzu, the leading early Taoist philosophers, who thought that harmony with nature could solve most of human beings' problems. A first Taoist answer to the question dominating this section, then, would be that we should view nature as the partner whose lead we should follow, the whole into which we should fit ourselves as compliant parts.

For Lao Tzu and Chuang Tzu, "nature" embraced the ten thousand things. They thought of animals, minerals, and vegetables as forming a single gestalt or patterned whole. Human beings, too, were but members of nature's single whole. Through all ranks of being, the force that guided nature, the *Tao,* worked its will subtly. Prosperity would come from seconding Tao, flowing in nature's train. Animals, minerals, and vegetables had no choice in this matter. They did what Tao prompted unthinkingly. Human beings had many choices, and so usually were somewhat the worse for wear. If human beings were wise, they would study the grain of nature and work with it, discern nature's veins and sculpt accordingly. Where the way of the world stressed *pa,* violent force, the way of nature encouraged *wu-wei,* active not-doing. Those who followed the way of the world came to grief, ever embroiled in strife. Those who learned *wu-wei* could hope for a ripe old age, filled with peace and dignity.

For Lao Tzu, nature was not to be sentimentalized. Often its ways stood at a great distance from human beings. Thus the description alluded to earlier: "Heaven and Earth are ruthless; to them the Ten Thousand Things are but as straw dogs. The Sage too is ruthless; to him the people are but as straw dogs."[2] With nature, things just go as they go. People are but part of nature's processes, so nature gives people no special exemptions. If a rock and a baby both lie in the path of a tornado, both will fly through the air. Nature has no qualms about applying the laws of physics, chemistry, biology, meteorology, and the like evenhandedly.

In nature, therefore, all things have a certain objective equality. The sage should imitate nature. For Lao Tzu, sentimentality about people can keep one from seeing what they really need. Neither for profit nor tender emotion should the sage fail to see what is there to be seen, fail to do what the facts say has to be done. This does not mean cruelty and bloodlust. It just means a calm detachment. Against the tendency of clans to make everything personal and volatile, the sage tries to reproduce nature's cool impersonality. Thus one can see him directing a group's resources to those who most need them, rather than to the wealthy or those who cry out the loudest. One can see him caring just as little for human opinion as the wind and the sky.

The Taoist sage comes to his peaceful objectivity by contemplating nature's behavior and contrasting it with human folly. Watching water wear away rock, he notices that gentle persistence accomplishes more than proud prominence. Seeing that a baby can dominate a household, she realizes that "power" is several-sided. It is the way of nature to go humbly, without fanfare, resembling the valley more than the mountain, the female more than the male. For Taoists true success is gaining an old age healthy in body and peaceful in soul. Who does not see that women have been the best Taoists?

Chuang Tzu, even more pointedly than Lao Tzu, sets human life under nature's direction.

> A child, obeying his father and mother, goes wherever he is told, east or west, south or north. And the yin and yang—how much more are they to a man than father or mother! Now that they have brought me to the verge of death, if I should refuse to obey them, how perverse I would be! What fault is it of theirs? The Great Clod burdens me with form, labors me with life, eases me in old age, and rests me in death. So if I think well of my life, for the same reason I must think well of my death.[3]

The *yin* and the *yang* are the "negative" and "positive" forces that ancient China thought composed all of reality (their different proportions accounting for things' different qualities). "The Great Clod" is Chuang Tzu's term for nature or reality taken as an ultimate whole. Just as a child should follow the directions of her parents, so an adult should follow the directions of yin and yang, the lessons that her inmost sense of things is trying to teach her. With time all human beings come to the verge of death. This is something to accept, nothing to fight. It is but part of the human circuit, which molds us from elements of the earth and finally returns us to compost.

Chuang Tzu therefore suggests that we should regard nature as a source of freedom. Attune yourself to the way things are, follow the changing seasons, and you will have peace. Put yourself out of tune with the way things are, fight the changing seasons, and your days will only bring you grief. Tao is much bigger than you, much deeper and stronger. It is silly to fight the way things are, especially near the end of your days. Then above all you must trust that the Great Clod will keep faith and give you rest.

WHY DO STATES FAIL TO FLOURISH?

Both Taoism and Confucianism articulated themselves as cogent philosophies during periods of Chinese history when civil strife was rampant. Consequently, both pondered deeply the problems of what we today would call political science or social philosophy. The differences in their responses to the problem of social dysfunction say a great deal about their distinctive identities as philosophical traditions.

Confucius bequeathed to his followers an ideal of *jen* (humaneness). In spending a long life as a tutor of upper-class young men and a would-be adviser to kings, Confucius taught that inner virtue and outer protocol could combine into a successfully functioning kingly rule. If the leader of a province were himself virtuous, the people would be drawn by his example. If the province kept the ancient rites exactly and beautifully, its people would regularly touch base with the cosmic powers drawing them to harmony. As well, they would regularly be schooled in the civic virtues that make social relations correct and just.

Lao Tzu and Chuang Tzu urged a more radical solution. In their opinion most of what passed for culture was more an impediment than an aid. Romanticizing the ancient past, they longed for a return to rougher days, when people had a better sense of nature's primacy and preferred silence to speech, simplicity to ostentation. Consequently, much classical Taoist speech is laconic and paradoxical, as though the masters wanted to exemplify how the great men of old would instruct the world in these later days. As Chuang Tzu pictured such men: "The true men of old slept without dreams, woke without worries. Their food was plain. they breathed deep. True men breathe from their heels. Others breathe with their gullets, half-strangled. In dispute they heave up arguments like vomit."[4]

Lao Tzu regarded "modern" laws the way Chuang Tzu regarded "modern" arguments: "The more taboos and prohibitions there are in the world, the poorer the people will be. The more sharp weapons the people have, the more troubled the state will be. The more cunning and skill man possesses, the more vicious things will appear. The more laws and orders are made prominent, the more thieves and robbers there will be."[5]

The problem with cultural adornments such as highly developed arguments and refined legal codes is that they tend to make us miss the point. The point is harmony with nature, deep peace that will make us at one with nature and able to live together equably. When we speak on and on, we tend to miss the deep silence of nature, the primordial spirituality out of which all insight and logic arise. When we keep refining our legal codes, we tend to miss the simple justice that all law codes ought to serve, the intuitive sense of fairness and compassion.

What, after all, are we really trying to accomplish with our speech? What is the end that all our laws should be serving? The end that all our laws should be serving is a strong, frugal, just social existence in which people can live unbothered by crime and not ground down by taxation. The end of our speech should be the truthful communication needed in social relations and the clarification of reality needed to grow more harmonious with the Tao. If education, rhetoric, or laws advance us toward these ends, they are good. If they prove to be detours or obstacles, they are evil. The Taoist sage has gone deeply enough into his own spirit, has consorted with nature intensely enough, to be ruthless in trying to cut out the falsity that most culture carries.

How, then, should the wise political leader proceed? Indirectly, subtly, like the Tao. Good politics is like cooking fish: the less poking and turning the better. Good politics honors the axiom, "Deal with the difficult while it is easy." It knows that unless we win our opponents' hearts, we have gained only a shallow victory.

The reason war and injustice are rampant throughout the land is that the influence of Tao has declined. Were people still simple, meditative, uncontentious, they would have many fewer problems. As it is, the best advice Chuang Tzu can give is to make oneself useless, like an ugly gnarled old tree. Useless as firewood, having only sour fruit, offering no lovely branches, the tree has survived intact to a fine old age. Had it been a carpenter's delight, or been bowed low with desirable fruit, or had just the bark for a wall hanging, someone surely would have cut it down or hacked away its limbs. The way to last out evil times, when governments rise and fall like the temperature, is to stay hidden, keep one's brilliance or virtues unknown. If you go parading off to court, like a new wizard sure to cure the economy or the army, chances are you will lose your head within the year. If you stay home, dragging your tail in the mud like a turtle, you will keep your head and enjoy many more sweet seasons communing with the Tao.

Overall, the most effective social doing is a not-doing. The greatest political action is a political passion. It is the gentlest of suggestions, the most artful of touches, that keep a society running smoothly. Barge in, order people about, impress your will forcefully and in the shortest of times you will set in motion forces of opposition sure one day to overthrow you. Bluster is not nature's way. Nature is wiser than that. States fail to flourish because neither their rulers nor their people fill themselves with nature's wisdom.

WHAT MAKES HUMAN BEINGS SAD?

If states fail to flourish because they lack the wisdom of the Tao, human beings become sad for the same reason. Not having lived in tune with nature, they come to their deaths with a sense of fear and regret. Where they could have enjoyed each day, accepting what Tao proposed and trying to flow in its wake, they have swum against the stream and so become deeply frustrated. Taoist therapy is mainly a matter of reversing one's spontaneous inclinations. Everywhere the world instructs us to strive and impress. Tao would have us go in just the opposite direction, practicing *wu-wei* and avoiding ostentation.

A section of the *Chuang-Tzu* (it is both a book and the name of an early Taoist) puts this teaching in the master's mouth as he is on the verge of death:

> When Chuang Tzu was about to die, his disciples began planning a splendid funeral. But he said: "I shall have heaven and earth for my coffin; the sun and moon will be the jade symbols hanging by my side; the planets and constellations will shine as jewels all around me, and all beings will be present as mourners at the wake. What more is needed? Everything is amply taken care of!" But they said: "We fear that crows and kites will eat our Master" "Well," said Chuang Tzu, "above ground I shall be eaten by crows and kites, below it by ants and worms. In either case I shall be eaten. Why are you so partial to birds?"[6]

Chuang Tzu comes to death with open arms, as one suspects he had come to each day since he had gained wisdom. He has open arms because his arms, his hands, his whole being is empty. He knows that the grasping never gain Tao's peace, the burdened cannot move lightly enough. He is free because his treasure is nothing so paltry as human riches or reputation. His treasure is union with Tao, soaring into the high heavens, cruising in the deepest depths.

There are many indications that early Taoists such as Chuang Tzu and Lao Tzu practiced spiritual regimes much like those of Indian yogins. (Later Taoists emphasized breath control, special diets, and sexual disciplines, in addition to their alchemical experiments in search of the elixir of immortality.) Thus when Lao Tzu counsels shutting the doors of the senses, or Chuang Tzu speaks of soaring like the giant birds of mythology, they probably are alluding to experiences that came through meditation and fasting. With the body anchored by breath control, the senses stilled and the mind peacefully collected, the Taoist could travel in spirit to wherever the Way beckoned him (once again, women were second-class citizens, although Taoism defended women against the worst Confucian misogynisms). This travel made him a prince, a diplomat, a sage according to the best of criteria—the experiential ecstasies that brought great joy to his soul.

So a more precise way of answering the question why human beings are sad is to say that they have reaped the fruits of their own distraction. Were human beings to gain control of themselves, practice meditation and the other interior disciplines, they could maintain courage in the worst of times, find peace and joy whenever the times were the least bit propitious. Extroverted people are at the mercy of every time and tide. When E. F. Hutton is about to speak they wait with baited breath. People who have mastered their own souls are substantially free. Knowing that their only legitimate master is the music of the spheres, they take secular affairs lightly, waiting for a fit of reason to strike the general populace and shake them from their habitual madness.

This madness, of course, is still a third reason why human beings are sad. So much in the world contradicts reason, justice, and peace that anyone having much to do with the world is bound to come home heavy-burdened. It is a sore mystery, human irrationality. In the days when the early Taoists flourished rulers went to war the way today's commuters head for the train station. Most of the people were peasants and their lives could be very brutal. Anyone with the intelligence of a Lao Tzu or Chuang Tzu was bound to consider society's sad state more than passing strange. Why should people slash and gouge one another? What great profit justified killing thousands of people in order to win a few more miles of scruffy territory? And why should a few people live high on the hog while many people barely scraped by? Seeing such madness, a person of sense was bound to turn away in disgust. It is no puzzle that Lao Tzu and Chuang

Tzu seem antisocial and reclusive. They had taken a hard look at the society of their times and come away sick at heart.

Our Western traditions orient us somewhat differently, but not so differently that the early Taoists' reclusiveness cannot seem an attractive option. We prepare to go to war as assiduously as the Chinese did 2,300 years ago, and our wars are immeasurably more destructive. A small fraction of our populations live high on the hog while a great many struggle below the poverty line. Between the nations of the North and the nations of the South the economic relationship is almost that of master and slave. So a person of keen eye and good heart is bound to be disgusted, just as such a person was in Lao Tzu's time. To counteract this sadness, she might shut the doors and retire within, leave the streets and ride her spirit through the heavens.

HOW SHOULD WE REGARD DEATH?

The picture of Chuang Tzu gently chiding his disciples overly concerned about his burial epitomizes how the good Taoist should regard death. Birth and death are equally natural moments in the cosmic scheme of things. From birth one takes materials from the vegetative and animal worlds (nourishment) and incorporates them into one's growing body. At death one returns this material to the general process, serving as other creatures' nourishment. Thus the "transmigration" that Chuang Tzu and other Taoists envision is not so spiritual as that of Hindus and Buddhists. China tended not to split the human person into a mind component and a body component, but to keep the single entity whole. What passed through nature's transformations was one's given stuff, one's bodily materials. If these were taken up by worms and roots, and so went into the lives of birds and fruit, they did not do so knowingly. It was not one's self that became a sparrow or a pear. Rather the Taoists held to a simple version of the law of the conservation of matter and energy. There is a certain amount of matter and energy dispersed among the Ten Thousand Things, and the changes caused by birth and death simply redistribute this matter and energy.

In a central sense, therefore, death was not a great evil. In a peripheral sense, however, death before one's expected time was a sizable cause for lament. As the religious Taoists' stress on gaining bodily immortality later showed, China has generally tended to prize long life. This is in part because long life allows one a lengthy old age, during which one may hope to consolidate a considerable fund of wisdom. Obviously wisdom would be good for the individual, but it also would be a boon for society at large. The extended family has been the rule in China, so grandparents have usually had a great influence. One hoped for a long life so that one could enjoy the respect and docility of many grandchildren.

The Confucians' reverence for old age led to extended observances of mourning. Indeed, gentlemen were expected to mourn the death of a parent for as long as three years. The mourning period was both a measure of the respect that a child was supposed to show its parent, the source of its life, and a socially sanctioned way (like a ministage in the Hindu life-cycle) for the mourning person to retire from active life and contemplate his own coming demise.

Chinese culture also made a great deal of family lines, not simply in the sense of the present members of the extended clan, but also in the sense of one's ancestors. After death a departed relative had to be appeased with sacrifices and little gifts, lest its ghost turn angry and trouble the household of the living. In *folk religion* the children of the deceased were obligated to keep making gifts, sending paper money or ceremonial food to their parents in the afterlife by way of fire. When the Christian missionaries came to China in the sixteenth and seventeenth centuries, they could not decide whether these Chinese attitudes toward departed relatives and ancestors were simply a matter of intense filial piety or were a kind of idolatry. The prevailing tendency to regard them as idolatry greatly hampered the work of adapting Christian faith to Chinese culture.

The classical Taoists tended to treat the seeds of what later became an elaborate ceremonial for death rather cavalierly. They were reconciled to the finitude of the human span and strove to maximize harmony with Tao in the present. Thus death served them as a constant pressure to be serious. If time is short, wisdom is all the more imperative. If each season has its place in nature's annual round, each season of human time should be used to its fullest. We should praise Tao for the energy of our children, enjoy Tao's dispositions of our own middle years (be they rich or poor), and accept Tao's taking of our loved ones through either normal or sudden death. Death above all is natural, a law imposed upon all living things.

Lao Tzu took some of these naturalist views of death and turned them in the direction of political wisdom, suggesting that the use of capital punishment is profitless:

> The people are not afraid of death. Why, then, threaten them with death. Suppose the people are always afraid of death and we can seize those who are vicious and kill them, who would dare to do so? There is always the master executioner (Heaven) who kills. To undertake executions for the master executioner is like hewing wood for the master carpenter. Whoever undertakes to hew wood for the master carpenter rarely escapes injuring his own hands.[7]

Thus we see the ultimate disposition of the Taoists: death is in Heaven's hands. The Tao will take care of punishment and reward, according to its own inscrutable canons. We know that we all must die, so in a certain sense we all already are punished. We would have better politics if leaders spent less time devising repressive measures like the death penalty and more time following the ways of Tao. The people would be better citizens if their leaders prized *wu-wei* more than they prized power maintained by force. For the person of vision, death is a great liberator. Knowing that one day it comes to us all, the person of vision fears no lesser human sanctions. Indeed, she is able to relativize even the arm of the state executioner. If we live deep in the Tao, we will regard death as a friend.

WHAT IS THE GREATEST EVIL?

It is hard to say what the classical Taoists considered the greatest evil. Ignorance of the Tao, with its attendant disorders, leaps to mind, but several other candidates beg consideration. First, the classical Taoists pilloried the evil rulers of their times, leaning hard on the Chinese sense of social solidarity to drive home the charge that an unjust ruler violated the mandate of heaven and so committed sacrilege. In such a situation, revolution was permissible, for the *te* or power mediated by the ruler (from heaven to the people) obviously needed a better conduit.

A second candidate was the Satanic sort of evil that Taoist priests later exorcized. An eyewitness account from modern times contains the following startling descriptions:

> [The priest] stopped and, taking an elongated ivory tablet, the symbol of wisdom and authority, he held it ceremonially in both hands in front of his chest and approached the bed slowly. There was a visible transformation on the energumen's [possessed person's] face. His eyes were filled with malice as he watched the priest's measured advance with a sly cunning and hatred. Suddenly he gave a bestial whoop and jumped up in his bed, the four attendants rushing to hold him. "No! No! You cannot drive us out. We were two against one. Our power is greater than yours." The sentences poured out of the energumen's distorted mouth in a strange, shrill voice, which sounded mechanical, inhuman—as if pronounced by a parrot . . . I had the impression that a pack of wild animals was fighting inside his body.[8]

The description adds other lurid details, in the spirit of the American movie *The Exorcist,* and amounts to a sobering look at demonic possession. No doubt other influences than simply those of the native Chinese tradition had shaped the witness's consciousness, but the Taoist priesthood has long contended with evil and exorcism has deep roots in the ancient shamanistic tradition.

Nonetheless this sort of Satanic evil is not prominent in Lao Tzu and Chuang Tzu. For them the disorders stalking humankind stem from the evil of neglecting the Tao. Perhaps it is hard for us to take this sort of evil seriously, accustomed as we are to social disorder, schooled as we have been to its constancy throughout modern (and other) history. We almost expect politics to be skewed, almost agree to the notion that ordinary human nature is depraved (as Alexander Hamilton put it in the 78th *Federalist* paper). The classical Taoists had no illusions about ordinary human nature, but they lived close to a time when the laws of nature were held sacred and thought to constrain human beings to virtue under the pain of being out of joint with sacred, ultimate cosmic power.

One can see this comparatively in Egypt, where *Maat,* the goddess and power of orderly virtue, was conceived as a sacred force running throughout the cosmos. The cosmos included human beings, as democratic fellow participants along with animals and gods. For human beings to violate *Maat* was to sin against the force that made everything be.

Something similar attached to the Taoist interpretation of the Way. For all the Taoists' wit and puncturing of pretense, they retained a great reverence for the Tao, a more than practical love. Tao was not just the code by which human beings ought to run their little affairs. Tao was the ultimate principle, the most basic or real meaning of things, and so something holy. Deep in the Taoist psyche lay the conviction common to most archaic peoples that the holy is the most real. To violate the laws, traditions, or good instincts that the Tao had fostered from China's beginnings was to shake one's fist at the best of reality's powers, pollute one's relations with the purest of beings.

The leading philosophical Taoists knew these things from personal experience of union with the Tao. Their meditations and ecstasies had shown them how the Way dwarfed all human conventions, how it opened the mystery of creation, the totality of the Ten Thousand Things. Those who knew Tao most intimately did not babble about it, because religious people never speak casually of holy things. Those who babbled almost assuredly did not know, because knowledge would have led them into silence. In their political prescriptions, therefore, the classical Taoists were expressing the compassion that union with the Tao had generated. Looking at the way that Tao-less rulers had led the people into misery, they felt moved at heart to try to lay out a blueprint for reconstruction. Their prescriptions stressed turning away from the going conventions and assumptions, turning back to Tao's preference for what was lowly, gentle, empty. Beyond this there was little they could advise, since all practical measures would depend on the prudence, the sense of fittingness, that only union with the Tao could foster.

So the worst evil, in the Taoist scheme, turns out to be waywardness, wandering off the only path that can make the individual or the state prosper. Disharmony or disunion with the Tao is dreadfully serious, because harmony with the Tao is our umbilical cord to all that is good. The person who misses the mark, failing to walk Tao's straight and narrow, is not for Taoists a "sinner." He or she is a dangerous fool, an object lesson in how not to live, how to waste one's lifetime and shame one's ancestors.

FIVE

A Buddhist View

HOW SHOULD WE VIEW NATURE?

Buddhism inherited from Indian culture a tendency to regard physical nature as somewhat unreal. In ancient India nature was generally considered by the philosophers to be part of *samsara* or *maya,* the levels of reality where the unenlightened give credence to plurality and separation. Insofar as nature offers us many potential objects of desire, nature also is a dangerous realm, a threat to our enlightenment and happiness. Probably human society is a more dangerous realm, since our desires for sexual pleasure, riches, and social status seem our strongest chains, but nature rightly remains suspect.

Thus the Buddhist holy man, like the Hindu holy man, was rather hard on his own body, the nature closest to him. The good Buddhist monk, for example, ate sparsely ("No stomach more than two-thirds full"), begged his food day by day, and lived a wandering life, settling down only during the rainy reason. His clothing was simple, his head was shaved, and he was schooled to discipline himself to minimal sleep and bodily comfort. All the world was burning, so it was imperative to control the body and liberate the mind.

When Buddhism emigrated from India to East Asia, it had to translate this stress upon the mind or spirit. East Asian culture, dominated by China, instinctively thought of the human person in holistic terms. Its preference was for the concrete rather than the abstract. One of Buddhism's most intriguing translations of its originally Indian religious scheme into Chinese terms occurred in *Ch'an.*

Ch'an (Japanese *Zen*) was the school that riveted the whole of the Buddha's message onto meditation. Rejecting complicated speculation and wordy discourses, Bodhidharma, the Indian holy man reported to have founded Ch'an in China in the fifth century C.E., insisted that only insight into one's own nature (which was identical with the dharma-nature of all reality) was of any significance. All else was indifferent or even dangerous. Thus Ch'an masters worked out regimes in which pupils strove mightily to break the illusions of selfhood, duality, and separation from nature. As these illusions departed, and enlightenment approached, the master could see in the pupil's whole bearing a growing integration. Mind and body now were working more harmoniously, pulling together rather than against one another. The person's posture, alertness, and energy all testified that spiritual health was on the rise.

Hui-neng, the Sixth Ch'an patriarch, expressed the further conviction that reality itself is spotless. Were we to see ourselves, nature, or any reality correctly, we would discover that imperfection and disharmony are only illusions thrown up by our ignorance. Hui-neng's rival had expressed how we ought to understand the Dharma as follows: "The body is the Bodhi Tree; the mind is like a bright mirror and stand. At all times wipe it diligently. Don't let there by any dust." This expression did not please Hui-neng. In response he gave his own interpretation: "Bodhi really has no tree; the bright mirror also has no stand. Buddha-nature is forever pure; where is there room for dust?"[1]

Following Hui-neng, we can say that we should view nature as spotless. In its own-being, nature is pure, because in its own-being nature is at one with Buddhahood. To *be* is to be filled with light, intelligible, ordered to mind. Mind is the bright mirror reflecting the lightsomeness of all that exists. Thus the Yogacara Buddhists, whose *Lankavatara Sutra* greatly influenced Ch'an, spoke of reality as "mind-only." Yogacarins, like followers of Ch'an, laid great stress on meditation. Exercising the center of their minds, they found reality to be completely mind-oriented, ideal, intelligible. Within every creature is a spark of the Teaching that founds and runs the world. The true meaning, identity, or being of any creature is this spark, this clarity *(bodhi)* that the enlightened person discovers.

In Japan such views led to the glorification of nature. Innately enlightened, nature was more perfect than human beings. Where human beings had to strive for their perfection, laboring painfully to overcome their dualisms and conflicts, nature serenely did what it had to do, expressed what it already was. There was no striving in the growth of an oak from an acorn. There was just a perfectly confident and simple self-expression. Imitating nature, the Zen warrior strove to make his swordsmanship or archery an unthinking expression of his integral, energetic mind-body.

Imitating nature, the Zen calligrapher strove to paint with "no-mind," no division between head and eye, head and hand. Japanese tea ceremonies and floral arrangements are similarly indebted to Zen notions of nature's perfection. Spare, understated, "empty," these art forms nourish the spirit by expressing nature's deep simplicity and graceful flow.

Perhaps the highpoint of East Asian views of nature, however, came in the landscape painting that flourished during the Sung Dynasty in China (960–1127). In these naturalist paintings emptiness is an achingly beautiful fullness. Elegant but minimal brush strokes suggest than an angular tree limb points to emptiness. A mist above a lake suggests the mind on the verge of enlightenment. A rock peak thrusting into the clouds is a sermon on nature's concrete perfection. In the Sung landscapes one can see the ineffable beauty that enlightenment discovers in nature. Were we filled with *bodhi,* we would view nature as a ceaseless manifestation of light.

WHY DO STATES FAIL TO FLOURISH?

In the Buddhist view, states fail to flourish because their leaders and citizens alike tend to be unenlightened. Leaders and citizens especially tend not to work hard at the great Buddhist virtues of compassion and nonviolence. Were a society to form itself by the precepts of not killing, not stealing, not lying, not committing sexual offenses, and not consuming alcohol, it likely would flourish. But the desire that drives most individuals drives most societies as well. If their leaders desire greater territory, societies will find themselves thrown into war. If their civil servants desire mainly their own gain, societies will find themselves riddled with corruption. These are the easy ways a people becomes disheartened and cynical. Both the Confucians and the Taoists thought that the ethical character of a state's leaders was of major importance. Buddhists could hardly have thought otherwise.

In his interesting book *What the Buddha Taught,* Walpola Rahula has transmitted the Buddha's notion of the "Ten Duties of the King":

> The first of the "Ten Duties of the King" is liberality, generosity, charity *(dana).* The ruler should not have craving and attachment to wealth and property, but should give it away for the welfare of the people. Second: A high moral character *(sila).* He should never destroy life, cheat, steal and exploit others, commit adultery, utter falsehood, and take intoxicating drinks. That is, he must at least observe the Five Precepts of the layman. Third: Sacrificing everything for the good of the people *(pariccaga),* he must be prepared to give up all personal comfort, name and fame, and even his life, in the interest of the people. Fourth: Honesty and

integrity *(ajjava)*. He must be free from fear or favour in the discharge of his duties, must be sincere in his intentions, and must not deceive the public. Fifth: Kindness and gentleness *(madava)*. He must possess a genial temperament.

Sixth: Austerity in habits *(tapa)*. He must lead a simple life, and should not indulge in a life of luxury. He must have self-control. Seventh: Freedom from hatred, ill-will, enmity *(akkodha)*. He should bear no grudge against anybody. Eighth: Non-violence *(avihimsa)*, which means not only that he should harm nobody, but also that he should try to promote peace by avoiding and preventing war, and everything which involves violence and destruction of life. Ninth: Patience, forbearance, tolerance, understanding *(khanti)*. He must be able to bear hardships, difficulties, and insults without losing his temper. Tenth: Non-opposition, non-obstruction *(avirodha)*, that is to say that he should not oppose the will of the people, should not obstruct any measures that are conducive to the welfare of the people. In other words he should rule in harmony with his people.[2]

In this listing of a ruler's virtues, we see Buddha's stress on the individual's conversion. It is not abstract matters of statecraft, semiscientific analyses of economics or politics, that interest the Master. It is what the person come to social power can do from his or her own virtue. Thus Buddhism has long tended to look to the dispositions of an ordered soul for society's healing. In this it is reminiscent of Plato, the father of Western philosophy, for whom the city-state was but the individual soul writ large. Put order in the individual ruler's soul, Plato said, and have that order obeyed by the populace, and you will soon bring the state to fine fettle.

Perhaps the most honored ruler in Buddhist tradition is Ashoka, a member of the Mauryan Dynasty, who ruled India from about 269 to 232 B.C.E. "From the Buddhist perspective he made his distinctive contribution by adopting the *Dharma* (the norm for religious morality) as the legitimating and guiding principle of his rule, and by giving special support to the Buddhist cause."[3] Historically, the main evidences of Ashoka's influence come from a series of edicts that he had carved on pillars and rock throughout his empire. In these edicts Ashoka repented of his previous militarism, expressed sorrow for the sufferings his wars had caused, and committed himself to the ethics of a lay Buddhist. If the edicts are factual as well as a piece of state propaganda, he renounced violence, prohibited the sacrifice of animals, strove for the toleration of all religious traditions, urged the bureaucracy to consider the welfare of all the people, appointed "dharma ministers" to look out for the public morality and provide social services, and initiated an extensive program of public works. In support of Buddhism Ashoka supposedly made pilgrimages to

Buddhist sites, refurbished a number of Buddhist burial mounds *(stupas),* supported and tried to unify the Sangha, and encouraged Buddhist missionaries to spread the Dharma, both within his own empire and beyond its boundaries.

Later legend expanded on Ashoka's merits, making him the greatest of the Buddhist kings. His refurbishing of stupas mounted up to 84,000 reconstructions, and he came to be considered the model for all Buddhist politicians to emulate. Theoretically, the major impact of Ashoka's model was that it gave a boost to the notion of acquiring merit through good deeds. This notion has become especially important in Theravada lands, furnishing the laity a strong motivation for conducting their secular affairs honorably. Thus a Buddhist might also answer this section's question by saying, "States fail to flourish because they have the misfortune not to be ruled by an Ashoka."

WHAT MAKES HUMAN BEINGS SAD?

Samsara is what makes human beings sad: the entire complex of suffering, death, and rebirth that we are condemned to endure, as long as we remain full of desire and ignorance. "All life is suffering," the First Noble Truth proclaims. There is no way we can avoid being sad unless we change our spontaneous outlook, reject what most of our fellow human beings are pursuing, and strike out after peace and joy. For this reason, many Buddhist gurus have thought that the best candidates for serious meditation and ultimate enlightenment are people deeply unhappy with their current way of life. Like the serious drinker who will not admit that he is an alcoholic, the person unwilling to face the dissatisfactions eating at his innards has not yet come to a burning thirst for a new life. It would be a mercy of the Buddha, therefore, to let his sufferings deepen. When he sees that he is a complete mess, he may finally be motivated to turn his life around.

Of course, determining what dissatisfactions are unacceptable and what are part of the fate that comes with being born demands no little wisdom. Nonetheless, Buddhists tend to think that any serious sadnesses come from our own ignorance and desire. Of itself reality does not have to be painful. Indeed, for the Sixth Patriarch there is nowhere any dust. The problem is not with our stars, but ourselves. If we do not have peace and joy within, we are seriously misguided. Peace and joy are always possible, for they necessarily overflow from a spirit that is enlightened. Not even disease or the loss of loved ones will take away our core peace and joy, if we are deeply enlightened. That seems to be Buddhism's calm claim.

How, then, do peace, joy, and enlightenment configure? First, peace is an inner order, the state of being realistic and so according things their proper value. Most of us are disordered, not according things their proper value, so most of us are somewhat upset, somewhat uneasy. For example, most people in Western societies worry about money. Their incomes are sufficient to provide them the necessities of food, clothing, shelter, education, and health care, but their jobs are insecure, or boring, or not as well-paying as they would like. Indeed, the Western societies constantly lure their citizens to want more commodities, more creature comforts, and so are in principle opposed to their citizens' personal peace.

Advertising, for instance, is largely an incentive to desire. Advertisers might defend their profession by saying that manufacturers have to make their products known, and consumers need to know of goods that may help them, but a great deal of advertisers' time and energy goes into trying to make their products desirable, trying to seduce potential consumers into feeling they cannot be happy without magenta nail polish, or a pork mcpickle sandwich, or a Muhammad Ali boxing glove. Thus Detroit has made the lissome blonde a standard adornment of noncompacts, and beer companies have staked a claim to the weekend. The image is the message, and the image says, "Buy me—I give pleasure."

One could write equivalent analyses of much Western work, education, and popular culture, showing how they depend on competition, dominance, and distraction in ways bound to disturb our peace. Where work might be as E. F. Schumacher described it, an expression of human beings' social and personal needs, in the current West it tends to be driven and mottled by the dollar, made a zone of profound dis-ease. Where education might be deeply contemplative, centered on understanding reality and appreciating its beauty, it tends in the current West to be in the service of business and the military, a matter not of gaining wisdom but of gaining greater technological control. Where popular culture could strive to bring all people the comforts of good music, art, and drama, it tends in the current West to exalt noise, sex, and superficial glamor, and so to be a prime enemy of the spirit.

These disorders wound us far more deeply than we realize, taking away great patches of peace. Similarly, they and the other disorders that are rampant snatch away our joy, which vanishes when our spirits become clouded. Joy is the sense of well-being we can only have when our spirits are clear and healthy. Put right order in a human spirit and joy will follow inevitably, as light follows the sun. Open the human spirit to the transcendent—to nirvana, Brahman, Tao, or God—and the spirit will breathe deeply, sense that this is the air for which it was made. That is why meditation is so important in Buddhist and other religious regimes. Meditation, or other forms of interiority, teach us experientially that we were made for much more than distraction and desire, that the best in us is much deeper and brighter. When we have open souls, pivoted upon the truth of the Dharma, we have joyous and thus satisfying lives.

The peace and joy we are discussing lodge deep in the human being, becoming quasi-permanent when one approaches enlightenment. They do not prevent physical suffering or emotional sorrow. They are not a cheap panacea or a thornless rosegarden. But they show that in our depths we human beings are stronger than the assaults of death and hate, our major enemies, let alone the assaults of our puny enemies, greed and distraction. So, we human beings are sad because we settle for puny rewards, a pygmy challenge, when we might become *bodhisattvas,* beings filled with light, peace, and joy.

HOW SHOULD WE REGARD DEATH?

From an analytic point of view, we should regard death as the breakup of the "heaps" that compose us, and as the point of transition between our present incarnation and our next:

> According to Buddhism, the death of any living being is inherent in its nature as a compounded entity: it is the dissociation of the constituent elements of a being. "For the born there is no such thing as not dying" (S.N., II). Death is thus a natural function of the ongoing process of life. For just as birth leads inevitably to a death, so a death leads inevitably to a birth. Of the five *khandhas [heaps],* the most important is consciousness. At the death of an individual these five khandas contract, so to speak, to a zero-point; the momentum of life itself, however, carries the constituent elements on beyond this zero-point, to open out into a new life; thus consciousness becomes associated yet again with another *rupa,* or form, another series of feelings, perceptions, etc. For this reason, the last state of consciousness of one's "life" is held to be of great importance for the first state of consciousness of the ensuing one; if it was a wholesome *(kusala),* this will produce a "wholesome" inauguration of new life. Similarly, if it was *akusala,* unwholesome, the ensuing new life will be unwholesomely inaugurated. It is not this last state only which determines the character of the new life; the whole previous life has produced a momentum of a wholesome or unwholesome kind, in varying degrees, which will inevitably have effects upon the ongoing course of life.[4]

This is a rather dry dissection, more appealing to the philosopher than to the ordinary religious seeker. It highlights the mechanics of death and rebirth, explaining them in terms of the ungluing of the heaps that finally explain us (since wisdom shows us to have no self). But it ignores both the ultimate cause of death (why is it that living beings are composed in this mortal way?) and most of death's personal significance. True, the description calls to mind the influence of karma, and suggests that the last moment in a given lifetime is especially important, but other Buddhists have meditated upon death more cosmically and more consolingly.

On the cosmic level, for example, some of the more idealistic Buddhist thinkers, for whom the Yogacara doctrine of "mind-only" held great appeal, have speculated that material creation itself only arose because of desire. Like a wind whipping up waves across what otherwise would be a tranquil ocean of being, desire introduced multiplicity and disharmony. From this multiplicity and disharmony came the various sufferings of the samsaric realm, including death and rebirth. When we root out desire, and gain the wisdom that goes beyond any tampering with the pure ocean of reality, we still the waves of multiplicity and suffering. In a sense, therefore, we return to the state that existed before the present material creation arose. "Before" in this case may not be a matter of time, but it is a matter of ontological (being) priority. So, to explain the present state of suffering and division, the idealistic Buddhists have to postulate a sort of "fall" from the ontologically prior state of nirvanic perfection.

Death is the spur that makes this sort of reflection personally pressing. Confronted by the certainty of our own dissolving, we should be driven to strive for enlightenment and release, as Gautama himself was. In the *Tibetan Book of the Dead* the notion that the verge of death and death's immediate aftermath were the prime opportunities for enlightenment generated a fascinating manual on how to die well. Utilizing staple doctrines of Vajrayana psychology, the *Tibetan Book of the Dead* portrays the lights and visions that the newly deceased may expect to experience, urging her to seize the great opportunity this transition-state affords and break with her karmic bonds once and for all.

From this and other traditional sources Philip Kapleau, an American Zen master, has compiled an interesting Buddhist contribution to the recent medicoreligious literature on death and dying: *The Wheel of Death.* When it comes to practical advice and rituals to aid the dying, Kapleau includes the following Buddhist prayer, adapted from the *Tibetan Book of the Dead:*

> O Compassionate Ones [Buddhas and Bodhisattvas], you who possess the wisdom of understanding, the love of compassion, the power of doing divine deeds and of protecting in incomprehensible measure: (such and such person) is passing from this world to the next. He is taking a great leap. The light of this world has faded for him. He has entered solitude with his karmic forces. He has gone into a vast silence. He is borne away

by the Great Ocean (of birth and death). O Compassionate Ones, protect (so and so), who is defenseless. Be to him like a father and a mother. O Compassionate Ones, let not the force of your compassion be weak, but aid him. Let him not go into miserable states of existence. Forget not your ancient vow.[5]

Summarily, therefore, we should regard death as both a goad to enlightenment and a time when we may make a great leap forward into freedom. If we have absorbed the Buddhist faith that there are many Enlightened Ones and compassionate Bodhisattvas, presiding over all the realms of reality, we may confidently call upon their aid, hoping that they will ease our passage from this particular existence and at least ensure that our next existence is propitious for salvation. Buddhist priests became the dominant functionaries in East Asian funeral rites largely because of this rich Buddhist fund of explanation and comfort regarding death. When East Asian people wanted to stop the painful wheel of death, they betook themselves to the saffron-robed representatives of the Dharma.

WHAT IS THE GREATEST EVIL?

From the foregoing, it is easy enough to see that Buddhists do not consider death the greatest of evils. As for Chuang Tzu, for mainline Buddhists death is part of the natural processes of samsara, a given along with suffering and rebirth. In the Buddhist scheme of things it is the causes of samsara that are the greatest evil: the desire and ignorance that keep us ensnared in a world that is burning.

Buddhism personified evil in the figure of Mara, the diabolic force who tried to thwart the Buddha's enlightenment, but this personification seldom gained the psychic leverage it had in some periods of Christian history (for example, the late Middle Ages and the early modern period), when Satanism and witchcraft were feared to be rampant. Buddhist lore regularly emphasizes that Mara was unable to prevent the Enlightened One's victory, concluding that his powers of greed, delusion, and hatred are circumscribed by Buddha's stronger peace, insight, and compassion. So too with the many goblins, ghosts, and lesser demons that populated folk Buddhism. Scary as they might be to the unsophisticated, they did not lodge at the heart of the religious enterprise, were not at all like the dark side of a Gnostic or Iranian dualism, in which the forces of darkness and light seemed quite evenly matched.

In underscoring the sufferings that flow from desire and ignorance, Buddhism could be quite concrete. Bodily pain, warfare, the great sufferings of animals, undue grief over death, and internal melancholy all derive from our deafness to the Dharma, our blindness to Bodhi's light. To grab our attention and turn us away from the blandishments of the world that incite our desire, meditation masters often proposed a close examination of how repulsive these blandishments are, when we see them as obstacles to enlightenment.

For example, Buddhaghosa, a fifth-century C.E. meditation master especially revered by the Theravadins, proposed lengthy exercises focused on the repulsiveness of food. To help meditators control their appetite for food (extinguish any undue desire), he counseled them to consider (1) that they have to go out to get their food, leaving their beloved solitude; (2) that they have to search for food by traipsing through muddy streets, often suffering abuse from the local villagers (from whom they would be begging); (3) that chewing food crushes it into a repulsive state, "like a dog's vomit in a dog's trough"; (4) that once food has been ingested the four effluvia (bile, phlegm, blood and pus) go to work on it, enhancing its unattractiveness; (5) that after ingestion food goes into the stomach, which "resembles a cesspool that has not been washed for a long time"; (6) that in passing through this cesspool food travels through malodorous regions traversed by the stomach's winds; (7) that digested food, far from being like gold or silver, gives off foam and bubbles, becoming excrement and filling the abdomen like yellow loam in a tube; (8) that digested food contains various "putridities," such as hair and nails, and if poorly digested can cause ringworm, itching, leprosy, eczema and dysentery); (9) that evacuated food is offensive and a cause of sadness; and (10) that both eating and excreting soil the body.[6] You might want to recall this little list the next time you head out for a gourmet meal.

Buddhaghosa and his colleagues developed similar meditations on other objects of desire, such as women. A beautiful woman, for instance, is "really" a bag of bones and foul odors. In a few years she will be a corpse and, like all corpses, will be full of maggots. Only a fool would bind himself more tightly to samsara for the sake of a few moments of pleasure with her. The same with anything else bodily. When we pay great attention to our bodies, whether in feeding, clothing, or adorning them, we distract ourselves from their fundamental mortality. Before long the body will be diseased and lie in the grave. Only the spirit is lasting. Only the spirit deserves our serious concern.

The minions of desire and ignorance, society's many distractions and false allurements, also come under Buddhism's attack. On the whole, however, Buddhism has balanced such attacks with a serene acceptance of the karmic realm, realizing that the majority of people probably always will be content merely to try to improve their karmic condition. Still, Buddhism has not hesitated to lash out against such species of desire and ignorance as warmongering, gambling, drunkenness, and governmental dishonesty. Indeed, more sophisticated contemporary Buddhist ethicians have taken traditional proscriptions like that against killing and given them broad social application. Thus Winston King's study of Theravada ethics quotes a contemporary Buddhist ethician who sees the precept of nonkilling as violated in "crowded and ill-ventilated buildings, workshops, and factories; slum conditions in big cities and towns; the overworking of children as well as adults; careless driving of steam boats, rail engines, planes, motor and other vehicles; sales of spurious medicines and adulterated foodstuffs"; and numerous other instances of social irresponsibility.[7] The greatest evil, the greatest cause of human suffering, is the greed and ignorance which spawn all our woes, from slums to nightmares of depression.

SIX

A Christian View

HOW SHOULD WE REGARD NATURE?

For Christianity, we should first regard nature as created. Nature is not an independent entity; it depends completely on God's good pleasure. God chose to create a world, from nothingness, only because the divine goodness wanted to diffuse itself. There was no lack in God that prompted the creative impulse, no desire to obtain an enhancement or supplement. In their being, all creatures point to the mystery of this divine generosity. If the most basic philosophical question is, as Leibniz and Heidegger suggested, "Why is there something and not nothing?," the most basic Christian answer is, "Because of God's mysterious goodness." On account of reasons we cannot fathom (since we cannot plumb the depths of a completely self-sufficient, infinite existence), God chose to share himself, communicate "outside," scatter a panoply of vestiges and images. In the beginning God created the heavens and the earth—because God is a prodigal lover.

Nonetheless Christianity has had some ambivalence about nature, and a strong tendency to subordinate the rest of creation to the interests of the human family. The ambivalence shows in biblical theology. On the one hand, God the creator gazes upon his work and finds it very good. On the other hand, the nations not loyal to the biblical God indulge in a fertility worship that exalts nature, causing the biblical theologians to fear that nature will become God's rival. So the Israelite prophets castigate the Baals and Astartes (nature deities worshiped by the Canaanites), stressing in contrast Yahweh's engagements with Israelite history, while the biblical psalmists incorporate nature into their songs of praise. God is both the Lord of history and the fashioner of heaven and earth. However, the biblical theologians feel safer and more comfortable with the themes of God's historical Lordship than with the divine presences in nature.

Jesus, a pious Jew, inherited this biblical theology, and Jesus' own preaching shows signs of continuing its ambiguity. On the one hand, Jesus manifests a loving eye toward nature, alluding to the lilies of the field, how beautifully they grow, and the sparrows who live carelessly. On the other hand, Jesus' major passion is for the will of his heavenly Father, which focuses on the Reign of God, the chance for the people to make a new start. Jesus does not seem uneasy with nature, or unaware of nature's beautiful revelations. But nature is not a major topic of his religious program, not a main referent of his prayer and ministry. As the Sermon on the Mount (Matthew 5–7) suggests, the main referent was the poor and dispossessed, whom the Kingdom of God would raise from semihuman status or marginality to the realization that God loved them as the apple of his eye.

Through subsequent history, nature has remained an important but less than innermost Christian category. The doctrine of creation slowly clarified to imply that God did indeed generate the world from nothingness, and the Genesis accounts of human beings' primacy among God's creatures (1:26–29, 2:19–20) sowed the seeds of a notion that human beings could use physical creation pretty much as they wished. Recently the ecological crisis has forced a reexamination of these and other religious factors in the history of humanity's treatment of nature, causing some commentators to accuse Christianity of a vicious *anthropocentrism*.[1] For example, where traditional people such as the American Indians tended to reverence nature as the sacred context of their whole lives, leading to the attitude that it would be sacrilegious to plunge the knife of a plow into the bosom of Mother Earth, medieval Christian peasants of northern Europe did not hesitate to develop huge plows to rip up the soil for vastly expanded farming.

The current outlook of many environmentalists therefore tends to make Christians sinners against nature, and (if the environmentalists are theists) to consider nature as a gift from God that human beings have badly abused. Historically, the equation frequently was reversed, nature being the more powerful partner. In the Christian lexicon, "natural evils" such as floods, earthquakes, and plagues did not make creation itself bad, but their destructive power impressed upon human beings the precariousness of their own creaturely situation. In times of fragile psychic balance such natural evils could be interpreted as scourges God was laying on to punish people for wrongdoing. In times of prosperity and mental health natural evils remained a caution against self-exaltation.

So did natural wonders remain a caution against self-exaltation, become an incitement to praise of God. Looking to the mountains, the seas, or the deserts, Christians in many centuries felt dwarfed by God's grandeur, cushioned by God's largesse. Like a huge medieval cathedral, the forest or the sea could put human affairs in proper perspective. We are simply people and our lives are very short. God is GOD, the eternal and almighty, and God's creation has vastly more in it than us human beings. Everything passes, but God and the stars remain. Looking to God and the stars, many sorely tried Christians gained a deep sense of peace. What would be would be, because human affairs subserved a vaster plan than any mere mortal could imagine. Thus, Christians often have said, we should view nature as a great sign of God's majesty, God's power, God's beauty—a great sign that human affairs are far from being the whole.

WHY DO STATES FAIL TO FLOURISH?

In the Christian scheme, natural evils are sobering but not ultimately shocking. Floods, earthquakes, and cancers are statistical possibilities, granted an evolutionary universe. There is no special malice in their occurrence, just as there is no special favor in the good genetic endowment that makes one's child a genius or one's family exceptionally long-lived. Through history, of course, the average Christian looked upon such natural occurrences as rather direct effects of God's action. Only since modern times has the notion of secondary causality distanced us from the biblical view, in which God is the direct cause of even natural phenomena. Still, nature has been rather faceless throughout Christian history, not a personified agent of influences we could label morally good or morally bad. It is social disorders that have eaten away at most Christians' souls, the carnage and injustice their own species has wrought.

States fail to flourish because of original sin. From the beginning, as the paradigmatic story of Adam and Eve in Genesis suggests, human beings have exalted themselves against God and set in motion forces of disorder. Set outside the garden of intimacy with nature and God, because of their disobedience, Adam and Eve watched their children contest and compete fratricidally. The parents had eaten sour grapes and the children's teeth were set on edge. Ever since this false start, human societies have struggled with murder, theft, and rape. All human beings are now born into a tilted game; none reaches maturity without having been seriously afflicted. So each generation has to learn obedience to God's will by suffering the painful effects of its waywardness. By the time they face the grave many people have made their peace with God, accepting the sovereignty of life's Mystery. Then their greatest pain becomes having to watch their children or grandchildren repeat the prideful pattern, since one cannot put old heads on young bodies.

In biblical terms human sinfulness directly expresses itself in idolatry and injustice. People self-concerned rather than docile to God tend both to worship their egos or bank accounts and to be unfair to one another. Pursuing mainly their own interests, rather than those of the collective community, they tend to neglect the widow, the orphan, any person shunted from the mainstream. For such extrinsic reasons as race, sex, or ethnic origin, they tend to deny other people's equal humanity, other people's equal imaging of God. Were they to face this equal imaging, and draw the obvious social inferences, they would have to give up their claims to special privileges, their accumulation of special luxuries or perquisites.

A root-going traditional Christian sociology would conclude that no one has the right to luxuries as long as anyone lacks necessities. The unity of the human family, the equal distance of all human beings from the glory of God, and the organic relation among the members of Christ's Body all pressure Christians to such an egalitarian view. But sin, human beings' deep tendency to miss the mark, blinds the mind and weakens the will, so unjust societies arise. When the sin is especially deep, such societies do not hesitate to throw the mantle "Christian" over their colonizing and raping. In the name of bringing a more elevating culture, they impose their will upon benighted pagans. In the name of subduing the earth and making it "prosper," they impose their will upon nature, polluting the seas and the air.

Stung by the criticisms of the modern socialisms, which themselves owe a great deal to Christian egalitarian ideals ("There is neither Jew nor Greek, there is neither slave nor free, there is neither male nor female; for you are all one in Christ Jesus," Galatians 3:28), contemporary Christian theologians have gone back to the Bible and retrieved the social critiques of the prophets. In so doing, some of these theologians have found a great deal of affinity between Marx and the Bible.[2]

When a society is set in justice, sincerely striving to give all its members equal access and equal opportunity, it is almost bound to prosper, since basic prosperity is living together supportively, cooperatively. In the main, nature is bountiful enough to provide us all an adequate living. The earth can produce enough food for a reasonable population, human ingenuity can provide sufficient technology to serve human beings the nourishment, clothing, shelter, medical care, and education they require. It is the greed and blindness of human beings that cause our famine and warfare. It is the disorders in human beings' souls that imperil the lives of billions.

On the margins of most societies live women, children, old people, and ethnic minorities whom a few self-assertive people have locked out of power and prosperity. In Christian social ethics, these few self-asserters have little basis on which to stand. The person who sees his brother and sister in need and closes his heart to them has no basis for claiming he loves God (I John 3:17). That was not Christ's way. Though he was rich, Christians recall, Christ emptied himself (Philippians 2:5–11) for the sake of his brothers and sisters. Ever since, fortunate Christians have had a strong obligation to serve the less fortunate. States fail to flourish because, through sin, people forget this example of Jesus. Averting their faces from God, they fail Christ's second command, refusing to love their neighbors as themselves.

WHAT MAKES HUMAN BEINGS SAD?

Negatively, human beings are sad because they are sinners, people disordered in spirit. Positively, human beings are sad because they intuit that the Spirit would give them grand measures of peace and joy, pressed down and overflowing, were they to order themselves aright. The shift from sadness to joy in the Spirit occurs through the process called conversion. So we may say that Christians consider human beings to be sad because they are as yet unconverted.

Through conversion, being turned around, people open their hearts to God, the loving mystery. In intellectual terms, Plato described conversion in the parable of the cave in the *Republic*. To begin the life of a philosopher, a lover of wisdom, one must leave the smoky obscurities of sense-bound existence and begin to contemplate the ideals that strengthen the life of the mind. As long as one is content with the intellectual or religious equivalents of rock music and pizza, conversion will not seem attractive. It is only when sensate existence fails to satisfy—to explain, strengthen against evil, root the soul in bedrock peace—that one is primed to move in other directions. Jesus has no gospel, no glad tidings, for people religiously complacent.

That is the point to Jesus' parable about the Pharisee and the tax collector:

> Two men went up into the temple to pray, one a Pharisee and the other a tax collector. The Pharisee stood and prayed thus with himself: "God, I thank thee that I am not like other men, extortioners, unjust, adulterers, or even like this tax collector. I fast twice a week, I give tithes of all that I get." But the tax collector, standing far off, would not even lift up his eyes to heaven, but beat his breast saying, "God, be merciful to me a sinner!" I tell you, this man went down to his house justified rather than the other; for everyone who exalts himself will be humbled, but he who humbles himself will be exalted (Luke 18:10–14).

So we might say that people are sad because they exalt themselves, whereas peace and joy come from exalting God in the core of one's heart. As long as we ourselves are the apple of our eye, the center of our lives, sadness is bound to afflict us. Parallel to the Buddhist teaching about selflessness, then, is the Christian teaching that she who would find her self must lose it. Like a dark patch placed across a window to block out the sun, the ego can block out the light and love of God. Thus Augustine, the greatest of the early theologians of the Latin church, described sin as love of self unto contempt of God. Conversely, holiness was loving God unto contempt (unconcern, disregard) of self. John the Baptist became a paradigm of this holiness when, discerning the significance of Jesus, he uttered the memorable words, "He must increase, but I must decrease." (John 3:30) That is the Christian notion of the way to joy: God must increase, egotism must decrease.

To be sure, many things in the life-cycle encourage the demise of egotism, and Christian spiritual masters have been quick to see them as providential. If we are to become mature we have to move to what Freud called the "reality principle," leaving the "pleasure principle" of childhood behind. If we are to gain a significant measure of judiciousness, we have to cut away our biases and emotional excesses, so that our minds can sit in tranquility, like a perfectly balanced scale. And if we are to die well, ending our race with a sprint, we have to make ourselves small, dispensible in the grand scheme of things. If a seed is to become a fine tree, it must fall into the ground and "die," losing its present form to gain a form much grander. That is the way the apostle Paul finally regarded death: The person of faith will put off his mortal body for the sake of a glorified, heavenly form.

Ours, however, is a psychologically sophisticated time, so objections to these notions of self-loss and "contempt" are almost sure to arise. Most of them will be met by noting that the loss of self that Christianity has urged should not lead to doubts, divisions, or self-hatreds. The basic Christian command to love others as we love ourselves implies that self-love has a noble status, while the different problems that powerless people suffer psychologically instruct us to deal with "ego" and "pride" delicately. Women, for example, may more often be afflicted with debilitating self-doubts than with overweening pride. Thus the paradigms developed by male spiritual masters may not fit women well, as the paradigms developed by white dominant classes may ill-fit blacks or Asians. The main biblical criterion of a healthy growth is the fruit that a course of action or a way of life is producing. When self-concern is sucking away our energy and joy, it is an enemy of the Spirit. When self-love is leading on to praise of God, willingness to suffer for what is right, it is a strengthening gift from the Spirit.

In the Christian view, we are happy, peaceful, and joyous when our spirits are open to the Spirit: ultimate reality, God. Anything less than ultimate reality cheats the unlimitedness of our drives to know and to love. So Christianity developed the "discernment of spirits," reading between the lines of sadness and joy to determine how God would lure his people.[3] Sadness meant separation from God, while joy meant the experience of God's presence at one's foundations.

HOW SHOULD WE REGARD DEATH?

In Christian perspective, we should regard death as the wages of sin and the threshold to a secure life with God. On this theme Paul wrote the definitive verse: "For the wages of sin is death, but the free gift of God is eternal life in Christ Jesus our Lord" (Romans 6:23). That we must die, and that death should shadow all our waking hours, is for Paul an effect and indication of our sinfulness, our distance from God. God is utterly alive, completely deathless. Were we intimately united with God, full partakers in God's life, we would be deathless. But we stand apart from God, clinging to our creaturehood in spurious independence. Thus our dissolution at death shouts of our folly. Like the Genesis (3:16–19) story of all the penalties that Adam and Eve accrued through their disobedience, our death is a myth holding the key to right relation with the mystery of creation. We suffer, must labor hard, and die because the mystery of creation, the love that makes things be, does not fill our minds, hearts, souls, and strengths the way it might, the way it wants to. Death is the wages, the merited payment, for our disobedience and alienation.

Nonetheless Christian faith says that God is wiser than our folly, stronger than our will to defiance, more creative than our genes for aging. So God has taken the fault of our sin and made it happy, a mechanism for passing over to heaven, the state of definitive union with the divine deathlessness and love. The only warrant for this peculiar faith is what happened to Jesus. Dying, Jesus destroyed death, the Christian fathers loved to say. Dying, Jesus went beyond the conviction of the Song of Songs that love is as strong as death, composing a new lyrical faith: Love is stronger than death. The love of the Father took Jesus' death and made it the gateway to unfailing life. The mystery of Jesus' resurrection is the fulcrum of history, the pivot, because there God revealed the transition from a creation mired in the grave to a creation inseparably riveted to its Creator.

Thus Jesus' death-resurrection was the crux of New Testament theology. For Paul it was a new passover, more ontological than the flight of the

Hebrews from Egypt, deeper through its conversion of the very structures of being from slavery to liberation. Where the Hebrews had toiled under the restrictions of pharaoh, all human beings have toiled under the restriction of death, an enemy regent dominating them from within. The escape that Moses led out of Egypt was a figure for all the liberation that Jesus' good news carried, especially the good news that death is no longer king. When Jesus descended into the grave, he took the liberating power of God into the depths of the netherworld, leading out of *Sheol,* the Hebrew realm of death, all the just spirits that had lived well with God. The strange appearances of Jesus after his death that the New Testament records are faltering, poetic attempts to portray this liminal, transitional period. They imply that Jesus was enough like his old historical self to enable his friends to recognize him, yet quite a new sort of being. Suffused with light, little bound by the space-time containers of this mortal realm, he exemplified the bursting vitality of God.

For John, the very Incarnation of the Word meant the coming of divine life to oust the powers of death, physical and spiritual alike. The Word's becoming flesh was like the drawing near of the *Shekinah,* the lovely divine presence, to pitch its tent in the midst of human beings once and for all. So the Johannine Jesus walks through time performing "signs" of the new heavenly life that has set out to defeat human evil and mortality. In the sign of raising Lazarus from the dead (John 11), Jesus discloses the glorious life of God that his own resurrection will place in history more dramatically, altering the course of time forever after. So Jesus says to Martha, Lazarus's sister, "Did I not tell you that if you would believe you would see the glory of God?" (11:40).

The second half of John's Gospel portrays Jesus' own glory in the architecture of the Cross. Raised up in apparent disgrace, condemned to the death of a criminal, Jesus shows the paradox of God's power, the weakness that bests Satan's strength. The "high priestly discourse" (John 14-17) suggests that Jesus' spirit dwelt in heaven, communing with his Father, long before his body was split on the Cross. The life of Father, Son, and Spirit, coursing in ineffable light, bathes Jesus' bloody brow with heavenly dew, sealing his flesh against the acids of decay.

In other parts of the Christian New Testament, and throughout subsequent Church history, the followers of Jesus continued to play with this central poetry. Knowing that the parabolic relations between death and life cannot be handled rationalistically, in the prudential ways of the business mind or the suspicious ways of the empiricist mind, they let their imaginations and subconscious instincts generate a wealth of images designed to tease the receptive, open interlocutor with the possibility that Jesus' resurrection broke open mortal history. "There," these images said in their dancing, allusive way, "there God showed that the love-power that made the stars wants to reach into our deepest tissue and save what is most ultimate in us from dissolution. There God pledged that, if we wish, we can make death a connection to an embodied life that will never end."

WHAT IS THE GREATEST EVIL?

As in Buddhism, in Christianity death is not the greatest evil. Satan and hell contend for that crown. Satan, the devil, is Christianity's most personal image of evil. For Christian mythology, Satan was one of the leading angels (beings of pure spirit), a great bearer of light. Satan refused to obey the good God of creation, however, saying, in his pride, "I will not serve." (In some versions of this myth Satan revolts because of God's plan to create human beings and endow them with the capacity for divine life.) For this disobedience Satan was cast from heaven, the realm of God, and placed in a realm of darkness and suffering. Together with his rebellious angelic allies, Satan has since presided in hell, trying to lure human beings away from God, to their utter ruin. The malice we saw in the Taoist exorcism could be matched by the malice that Christian exorcisms have encountered, suggesting that something in the human psyche and/or external reality hates God and human well-being.

Hell is the definitive achievement of alienation from God, the polar opposite of heaven. Where heaven implies that human beings have found the fulfilling good for which their hearts have been made, hell implies that human beings have missed this fulfilling good and so come to complete frustration. Christian imagination has embellished hell with fire and brimstone, racks and thumbscrews, and other signs or instruments of suffering, but the core of the notion has been separation from God, loss of the one love-relationship that creatures have been made to attain. To be bereft of God has been considered the ultimate suffering, prefigured in an earthly life focused on self or unfulfilling creature comforts and made definitive, unalterable and eternal, in hell.

The Christian view of evil therefore assumes that human beings have a significant freedom. God makes an offer of love, a self-gift and revelation, and human beings are free to accept or reject it. They are free to ruin themselves, choosing what is for their own destruction, rejecting what is for their own fulfillment. That is the "mystery of iniquity," the deep absurdity of sin. In choosing what ruins themselves as individuals, people also choose what ruins their lives together, what renders human community impossible. The sin that "Satan" prompts is lovelessness, division, brutality. It reaches technicolor form in the death camps of Nazis, the mindless savageries of war, the wholesale degradations of slavery. The Vietcong soldiers who drove chopsticks through the eardrums of little first-graders so that their families would not oppose the "liberation" of Vietnam gave Satan human faces. The American soldiers who went into Vietnamese villages like My Lai butchering families of civilians were similarly diabolic. Shockingly, human beings can have fits of madness in which they love doing evil, enjoy killing and giving pain. That is what Christianity has sensed to be farthest from God the good Creator and so labeled utterly hellish.

For Christian faith, however, even the greatest evils do not defeat God. As the New Testament shows Jesus fighting with Satan and conquering him from the Cross, so Christian theology as a whole teaches that where sin and evil have abounded, grace and goodness have abounded the more. There is no parity between good and evil in the Christian scheme of things, no equality. In creating, God poured forth light and life. The explosions of the stars say that the source of the universe is powerful and lightsome. The play of otters and dolphins says that the source of the animal world is a joyous free spirit. And the minds and hearts of human creatures, what do they say about God? For the Christian tradition they say that God is light in whom there is no darkness at all, that God is only love.

Thus Augustine, who had been a Manichean, believing that good and evil were two equal principles contesting throughout all reality, moved to Christianity and "solved" the problem of evil by showing that evil is essentially a privation of good. Evil is not something positive in itself. It is disorder, lovelessness, the failure to do what one should. Physical or natural evils are the aberrant growth of cells, the imbalance of atmospheric forces, the disturbances in the regular tides that cause ecosystems to fall out of homeostasis. Moral evils or sins are the irrationalities and passions that cause people to choose badly, lash out hurtfully. There are no positive beings labeled "evil," no creatures composed utterly of surdity and hate. Evil is not creative but destructive.

So evil does not come from God except permissively. God has accepted the possibility of natural evils, in making a universe (of such splendor) according to statistical laws. God has accepted the possibility of moral evils, even diabolical sins, in making creatures free enough to accept his love and enter into personal relationship with him, free enough to appreciate one another and lay down life for their friends. So did Augustine reason, exonerating God from the accusation that creation included evil members. So did the author of the book of Job argue, going beyond God's exoneration to the accusation of us human accusers: Who are we to say how the universe ultimately weighs out "good" and "evil?" Where were we when God gave the universe its program, when the morning stars sang together and all the good angels shouted for joy? The greatest evil is forgetting our creaturehood, trying to play God, and so rejecting the love that can make us wise, free, and immortal.

PART THREE

God

PEOPLE living in the West tend to equate religion with God. However much their actual church or synagogue life may be shaped by social dynamics, peer attractions and peer pressures, they tend to think that the center of their religion is God, the personal creator who made the world, the personal judge who will scrutinize their lives and render a verdict of guilty or innocent. It comes as something of a shock, therefore, for Westerners to learn that people in other parts of the world have not believed in a personal creator or judge in the same way.

For example, the hunting and gathering cultures that have left traces in the world views of such contemporary peoples as American Indians, Africans, Eskimos, and native Australians largely reverenced the power of nature. For them a sacred force ran everything in the world, and good living was gaining and keeping harmony with this force. So one was reverent toward the directions of the compass, the winds and the waters, the animals and the plants. Father Sky and Mother Earth were especially important, but the totem (guiding animal spirit) of one's particular tribe — beaver or elk, bear or eagle — also deserved special attention. Nature was alive with power, and all of nature's power could be holy.

Most ancient peoples therefore did not have a single personal deity. Nor did most peoples of the East. Confucian Chinese, for example, inherited the notion of *T'ien,* a heavenly overseer, but T'ien usually was quite impersonal and distant. *Shinto,* the native tradition of Japan, was largely a nature religion focused on the *kami,* the spiritual power of life manifested in tall trees, striking rocks, or other unusual natural objects. Ancient Indian religion, as we have seen, moved from the pantheon of natural gods

83

enumerated in the Vedas to the impersonal Brahman and Atman of the Upanishads. Theistic Hinduism, worshiping Krishna, Shiva, and numerous mother goddesses, put a more personal face on divinity, but with much less specificity, much more flexibility, than Westerners showed in dealing with their Adonai, Christ, or Allah. "God" or "Divinity" therefore admits of multiple denotations, if one builds the notion from the broad base of humanity's actual experience up to the most resolutely monotheistic traditions, rather than from the monotheistic traditions alone.

In this book "God" has to cover the whole spectrum of humanity's designations of ultimate reality. Sometimes in confusion, occasionally with blinding clarity, human beings have groped after the sacred reality founding their world and generally have found it. Historically, virtually all people have believed in an ultimate power transcending the human realm. North and South, East and West, traditional humanity has stood in awe of nature's creative and destructive powers, has wondered deeply about human spirituality, and has been brought to its knees by the experiences of birth, love, suffering, and death. Everywhere, traditional humanity has found life to be mysterious: richer, fuller, more demanding and absorbing than what human or lower-level causes could explain. So everywhere traditional humanity has looked beyond the human level, reaching up to the heavens or down to the under-earth, for an origin and destiny that were "more."

In modern times, beginning in the European West, this traditional assumption or faith in transcendent, superhuman powers came under critical attack. As human beings developed the awesome rational strategies that generated modern science and technology, many came to doubt that "God" was a necessary hypothesis. As evolutionary and psychoanalytic insights came on the scene, much in the traditional religions seemed unprogressive or neurotic. The extremely defensive reaction of the Western religious establishments to the advances of modern science only strengthened intellectuals in their suspicion that religion was a bastion of superstition and psychological weakness, and when the socioeconomic critiques of Marx and the other political reformers joined the assault, most Western intellectuals thought religion was on the ropes.

Today, in what many call a post-modern time, religion has made something of an intellectual comeback. Since several centuries of post-Enlightenment progress have not brought a world of profound justice and peace, most fair-minded people are now willing to look again at the ancient traditions' religious wisdoms.[1] In the wake of just this century's wars, and in the light of the next century's nuclear dangers, we need all the help we can get.

Joining this post-modern sense of a need for review to a historian's

understanding of humanity's long religious past, Wilfred Cantwell Smith
has recently castigated those who cling stubbornly to the modern notion
that God or the transcendent is meaningless:

> "One of the advantages of familiarity with the world history of religion
> (of man) is that one is then not intimidated by current Western trends
> of thought that see this as a "problem." Rather than feeling called upon
> to defend this awareness of what some of us call the divine before the bar
> of modern skeptics' particular logic and exceptional world view, I am at
> least equally inclined to call them before the bar of world history to
> defend their curious insensitivity to this dimension of human life. Seen
> in global pespective, current antitranscendent thinking is an aberration."[2]

In Part Three we look at the unaberrant, immensely influential dimension of transcendence in Buddhism, Christianity, and Islam.

SEVEN

A Buddhist View

WHAT DO WE MEAN BY GOD?

By and large, Buddhism has not pivoted on what Westerners call God.
There has not been a personal creator at the origins of the Buddhist world,
nor a personal judge or consumator at the end of the Buddhist world.
Originally, Buddhism accepted the Indian notion of transmigration, and
the Indian extension of this notion to a universal system of creative
expansion and contracting decline. The great ages (*kalpas*) of Indian cos-
mology gave the universe a pulsating structure. (In classical Indian thought
a kalpa measured 4,320,000 human years. Each kalpa divided into four
ages, the best of which was a golden age and the worst of which was the
sin-ridden present. A thousand kalpas made a Brahma Day, which was
the span from the universe's creation to its destruction. This was followed
by a Brahma Night, a period of universal rest lasting the same time as a
Brahma Day.) Thus the universe waved out and rushed back in immense
pulsations. This was simply its nature, its law. No personal force above
the universe directed the universe's pulsations or could stop them.

Buddhist nirvana was a state outside the realm of the universe's pulsations. If a person snuffed out desire, he or she escaped the great karmic
or samsaric cycles of birth and death, Day and Night. So nirvana came
to possess qualities transcending any possessed by karmic beings. Although the Buddha himself was quite laconic about nirvana, preferring to
try to bring people to it rather than lecture them about it, and although
the subsequent Buddhist tradition retained some of the Buddha's reti-
cence, nirvana yet was generally understood to possess a stability, light,

and fulfillment that samsara never afforded. In this way, nirvana became what we might call "ultimate reality," samsara's foundation and fulfillment. As such, it possessed some of the attributes that European philosophical theologians accorded their God.

Thus some aspects of what we Westerners usually mean by God (stability, light, bliss) have often been found in the Buddhist nirvana. Other aspects have often been found in the Buddhist *Buddha-nature* or *Dharmakaya*. The Buddha-nature is the enlightenment that Gautama achieved transposed into the substantial nature or essence of all things. The light or intelligibility of things that Gautama grasped and manifested became, through the philosophers' steady musings, the inmost reality or "suchness" of everything that exists. When Buddhists further reflected on the correlations between the historical Buddha and this universal intelligibility, and between the historical Buddha and the different heavenly realms that Buddhist religious imagination came to picture, the doctrine of the three "bodies" of the Buddha arose.

The first body was that of the historical Buddha, Gautama. The third body was that of the Buddha as the presider over all the realms of heaven: the glorified body. The second body was that of the Buddha as the inmost intelligibility or light of all creation: the Dharma-body or Dharmakaya. This second body was quite akin to the Christian Logos—the Word that gives all creation its order and meaning. Insofar as "God" has meant to the West the ultimate source of meaning or intelligibility in the world, the one who guides the world providentially and stands behind the order in nature, the Buddhist Dharmakaya has approximated the Western sense of God the Logos.

However, when we let Buddhists use the word God on their own, not seeking similarities to Western usage, we find that they have taken over Indian or East Asian notions of divinity and so tended to think of many less than ultimate forces ("gods") having an influence on human life. The Buddha himself accepted the gods of Indian religion, but he thought that they were not the key to enlightenment: "The Buddha realized that men cling desperately to anything which they believe might deliver them from the wreck of time, decay, and death. They cling to the gods as though the gods will persist when all else disintegrates. But the insight of the Buddha was that there is nothing but the process of change and decay and again-becoming which carries all with it. There is nothing apart from the process and nothing within the process which can endure."[1]

For Gautama himself, therefore, the gods were of little importance. The key to enlightenment and escape from suffering lay in rejecting desire and embracing the Eightfold Path. After the Buddha, however, devotional Buddhism came to reverence certain bodhisattvas or saints in ways that parallel the Hindu bhakti reverence of Krishna and Shiva, the Christian love of the infant Jesus or the Sacred Heart. Thus in East Asia the bodhisattva *Kuan-yin* became, in effect, a mother goddess, to whom great numbers of Buddhists had recourse for good health or the birth of a child. In Tibet *Tara* functioned similarly. Scriptures arose that reverenced Gautama himself as a raincloud of light and mercy, a universal savior, while other Buddhas such as Amida (and scriptures such as the *Lotus Sutra*) became the central religious focus of devotional sects.

Overall, therefore, the question of Buddhist theism is rather complex. If we mean by "God" a personal creator of the world from nothingness, Buddhism is not theistic (would not sanction using "God" that way). If we mean an object of ultimate concern, especially one prayed to personally in hope of love and favor, popular Buddhism frequently has been theistic, frequently would sanction our saying, "There is a kindly high power to whom I entrust my life, from whom I beg good fortune, and if you wish you may call this a God."

WHERE IS GOD IN OUR LIVES?

Buddhist divinity in the sense of nirvana is everywhere in our lives, according to the Mahayanists who came to equate nirvana and samsara. What is relative, fleeting, painful, and selfless can only stand, exist, on the basis of something other, something of an entirely different, transcendent order. We cannot say a great deal about this "other." Our best approach to it is negative: not-painful, not-fleeting. But enlightenment shows it to be utterly, primordially real. It is not a state, not a thing, not a substance. It is reality seen in light of the wisdom-that-has-gone-beyond to be undivided, flowing, and full of light. It is the reverse of the condition that ignorance and desire cause us to suffer. So, divinity or ultimate reality in the sense of nirvana is everywhere, but only for the wise. It is the inmost being, the bodhi-nature, of all existents, but only for the bodhisattvas, the wisdom-beings who see things as they really are.

The Awakening of Faith, an important Mahayana treatise, discourses on some of these matters in describing the mental aspects of ultimate reality: "The essence of Mind is free from thoughts. The characteristic of that which is free from thoughts is analogous to that of the sphere of empty space that pervades everywhere."[2] Thus ultimate reality is like a great mental light, deeper and purer than any individual thoughts, that shines everywhere, like the matrix of space in which all things are set. Images such as these probably made little sense to the Buddhist laity, but they held great appeal for philosophers and meditation masters. It appears that for them divinity was especially prominent in the mental portions of life.

The Buddhists who meditated regularly and pondered the scriptures became sensitized to the likely presence of the Buddha-nature or Dharmakaya in consciousness or thought. For schools such as the Yogacara, reality itself was mind-only, and when one grasped this truth, by seeing that everything which is is mind-oriented, holds out the possibility of being understood, one has located a prime presence of divinity, ultimate reality.

Ch'an and Zen utilized a meditational focus to develop a life-style that sought enlightenment, ultimate reality, by living out the interconnectedness of all reality. Especially in the Soto school of Zen, one sat in peaceful meditation, trying slowly to help one's deep, original bodhi-nature emerge. Where the Rinzai school of Zen vigorously assaulted the mind's misconceptions, using techniques such as puzzling *koans* (paradoxical sayings such as "the sound of one hand clapping") to get beyond ordinary logic and penetrate reality as a whole, Soto tried peacefully to focus the mind and let all of life become more and more graceful. Thus the contemporary Japanese *roshi* (master) Shunryu Suzuki told American aspirants to Zen enlightenment that it was a matter of getting to the "beginner's mind" that could see reality freshly, as a constant series of new wonders, new expressions of basic reality's freshness and light.[3] For the person unwarped by tired mental conventions, the clear light of reality was dancing everywhere.

Theravadin Buddhists of recent times also have stressed that meditation is a fine way to penetrate reality's ultimate nature.[4] Drawing on a long tradition of keen psychological commentaries, masters in Burma, for example, have stressed the difference between Hindu yoga and Buddhist meditation. Where yoga has stressed a certain emptying of consciousness, so as to experience trance (*samadhi*), the original Buddhist tradition that these masters are trying to revive stressed insight, illumination. Following the stream of one's consciousness, and coming to grips with one's present feelings, one gradually gains mastery over the functioning of one's mentality and purifies it, so that the noble truths of the Buddha become internal and self-evident. The result of this process of self-observation, purification, and realization is a flood of light and the removal of one's sense of suffering. For the comparative scholar of religion, this experience begs classification as an encounter with the divine.

Last, we may say that the majority of Buddhists—in Theravada, Mahayana, and Vajrayana alike—probably have found the divine or ultimate through devotional exercises focused on a bodhisattva, goddess, or religious text. Melford Spiro's *Buddhism and Society*[5] offers rich details on the religious lives of lay Burmese Buddhists, showing how the divine has been present to them through household and village rituals. Similar studies of the laity in the Tibetan or devotional Japanese sects would probably show similar results: a stress on local and family prayers, shrines, festivals, or imaginative contemplations of deities.

Thus we ourselves have watched Shin Buddhists in present-day Kyoto gather on Sunday morning to hear scriptures chanted, recite prayers, and listen to a sermon. Similarly, we have watched ordinary people come to the shrine of Kannon (Kuan-yin) in Tokyo to pray for a fruitful pregnancy. With flowers, incense, and rhythmic chanting, Buddhists everywhere have sought to engage their senses in the worship of their chosen Buddhist deity. With constant repetition of such refrains as "Greetings to Amida" they have tried to fill themselves with what the West has called "God-consciousness." Thus divinity can be many places in the Buddhist's life—wherever serious effort, concentration, and openess to reality's ultimate light point her.

IS THERE A PRIVILEGED WAY TO GOD?

The way to God obviously depends on one's sense of where God is, so the different Buddhist schools have stressed different paths as their varying senses of God's "location" have suggested different approaches. Zen, for example, has sought the realization of ultimate reality largely through meditation. Vajrayana sects usually have employed techniques from the tantric tradition that stress imagination and psychosomatic energies. Nonetheless, all Buddhists probably would agree that the triad of meditation, morality, and wisdom is essential to the flourishing of Buddhist religion and so constitutes the main highway to divinity.

Depending on one's point of view, each of the three legs of this tripod can claim a privileged status. Meditation, for example, is the exercise that most directly changes one's consciousness and actualizes the bodhi or wisdom-nature of one's own being. Where morality is essential for disciplining the passions and achieving social peace, and wisdom or philosophy is essential for mastering the Buddhist conception of reality, meditation allows believers to actualize the light within themselves, the unsullied nature there from the beginning. When this unsullied nature emerges into full realization, all the puzzles of the Dharma are solved. Standing beyond the ignorance that afflicts ordinary humanity, the enlightened person sees the truth of the Buddha's Four Noble Truths, the correctness of the Eightfold Path, the profundity of the Three Marks that the community has long found to characterize unenlightened reality. What once was taken on faith is now a matter of personal knowledge. Where reality used to be plural and divided, now it seems of a single lovely piece.

Morality or ethics approaches enlightenment and nirvana by way of behavior. Disciplining the body, mind, and social instincts, Buddhist morality asks for a heartfelt obedience of the five basic precepts. The person who does not kill, steal, lie, transgress sexually, or drink intoxicating liquors is preparing her- or himself for a break with samsara, the realm of desire. As well, she is preparing a good social life, a generous membership in the Sangha or general community. Embracing *ahimsa,* the will not to injure any living thing, the Buddhist grows sensitive to the great suffering that creatures endure everywhere, vowing to do something practical to alleviate it. Developing *mahakuruna,* the virtue of great compassion, the Buddhist is drawn to the bodhisattva vow to labor for the salvation of all living things. Politically, ahimsa and mahakaruna could move a person in the direction of great social justice and service. Ecologically, they could move a person to a deep appreciation of the interconnectedness of all living things, a deep appreciation of our responsibility not to injure the other citizens of the earth. These virtues have not always flourished in Buddhist history, not always produced the charitable institutions one might expect. But they have been a great force for good, a strong presence of the divine.

Wisdom or philosophy is not for Buddhists an academic affair (although there have been great Buddhist universities, for example in Tibet). Rather it is another way to nirvana, another path of deliverance from samsara. Through studying such bodies of wisdom literature as the Prajna-paramita sutras, intellectually oriented Buddhists have tried to grasp the fleeting character of nonenlightened reality, the dance of all the dharmas (component entities of reality), both mental and physical. From earliest times the Abhidharma literature that one can now find in the Pali canon of scriptures pursued this religious path. In Mahayana the Prajna-paramita literature arose to depict how reality looks when one has passed beyond samsaric views, fostering such challenging philosophies as that of Nagarjuna, leader of the Madhyamika school, who wrote dazzling logical assaults on the ordinary misunderstandings of Buddhist doctrine and spotlighted the centrality of emptiness.[6] The philosophers developed their treatises in the context of meditating intensely and trying to live in full obedience to *sila,* Buddhist morality, but for them the privileged way to the divine or ultimate was the use of their dialectical, razor-sharp minds.

A fourth way to ultimate reality stands clear in the living Buddhism of today's East Asia. This is the way of beauty, the Chinese and Japanese blending of religion and aesthetics. The Japanese tea ceremonies, flower arrangements, shrine adornments, and the like, for instance, represent the melding of the Shinto and Buddhist convictions that nature offers us harmony and peace of soul, if we approach it correctly. Harmony and peace of soul further suggest the Buddhist notion of emptiness, freedom from grasping desires and agitated thoughts. Wandering the Buddhist shrines of Kyoto, one sees numerous variations on this theme. For example, at the Moss Temple one imagines the divine as a bank of green velvet, shaded with endless variety, or as a quiet stream wandering between restful rocks and trees. At the Temple of the Golden Pavilion one sees a perfect lake mirror a perfect pagoda, both delighting one's eye and taking one's breath away. At the Rock Garden Temple angular stones obtrude into bare raked sand, expressing how each individual being both breaks forth from emptiness and points back to its empty source. Contemplating any of these beautiful scenes, one realizes that East Asian Buddhism has conjoined the ultimate or divine with the beautiful in arrangements that hush the soul to grateful appreciation.

OF WHAT USE IS RELIGIOUS RITUAL?

The Buddha himself seems to have felt that religious ritual has limited value. Since he had not found the Hindu sacrifices of his day helpful in his own quest for enlightenment, Gautama could hardly be expected to lay great stress on equivalent ceremonies for his followers. Sufficient for his followers would be the Dharma of the Four Noble Truths and the Eightfold Path. If a person joined the Sangha and pursued a complete understanding of the Four Noble Truths, a wholehearted walking of the Eightfold Path, he or she could expect to make great progress, could hope even to attain a complete break with suffering.

Still, the Buddha somewhat ritualized his own days, in that (tradition reports) he regularly rose at daybreak, washed, and sat in meditation until it was time to go begging for food. (He would stay close enough to a village to facilitate this begging, but far enough away to assure himself of peace.) After eating lightly, he would instruct his benefactors in the Dharma and then return to his residence to wash and rest. Next would come preaching to his monks and responding to any monks who came to him for individual guidance. Then would follow another rest, preaching to the laity, and a cool bath. The evening would be devoted to individual conferences, after which (the pious sources say) the Enlightened One would instruct any gods that came for help.

Despite this regularity, there is little indication that the Buddha himself chanted, danced, or prayed to any divinities. Before long, however, his followers collected his sermons and made them the main ingredients of ceremonies venerating the Buddha's wisdom, begging the Buddha's aid, or recalling the essentials of the Buddha's religious program. Monks organized themselves under teachers who regulated their days, assigning them periods of meditation and periods of work, time for rest and time for individual conferences. Laity began to assemble regularly at Buddhist temples for sermons, chantings of the Buddhist scriptures, recitations of key Buddhist doctrines, and the like that would help them refresh and deepen their commitment to the Buddha, the Dharma, and the Sangha (the three "jewels" of Buddhist faith). Insofar as incense, flowers, and music adorned these ceremonies, they became, like the rituals of other religious groups, efforts to engage the whole person, mind and body, senses and soul, with the Teaching.

Nonetheless Buddhism has not poured its religious reality or truth into sacramental rites the way that other religions, especially Christianity, have. The ceremonies commemorating the Buddha's birthday, the New Year, or the death of a family member were not so much enactments of the Dharma, "bodies" in which the Dharma could become present, as stimuli to remember the Teaching and the consolations it carried. Among the several religious traditions that simultaneously formed East Asian society (Confucian, Taoist, Shinto, and sometimes Christian or Muslim), Buddhism has stood out for its control of funeral and burial rites. Apparently East Asians have found the Buddhist notions of transmigration and karma the most persuasive explanations of death and the afterlife, as they have found the Confucian notions of political organization the most persuasive teachings about family and social life.

In some ways meditation has served many individual Buddhists as their main religious ritual. By sitting regularly in concentration, the individual Buddhist could prove her or his commitment to the Enlightened One and strive to appropriate the Teaching that the faith said held the key to happiness. Serious meditators have usually had a teacher, who furnished both the theory to guide the meditation and the counsel to evaluate its course, and through the teacher (who usually has been a monk) the meditator has formed a strong link to the monastic center of the Sangha. But the main benefit of meditation has been its regularizing the individual's efforts to achieve enlightenment. From this central daily activity, even if it only lasted half an hour, the rest of the day could take shape. The rest of the day then became a testing ground, on which the serenity and truth generated by the meditation could be challenged, evaluated, and deepened.

The use of religious ritual, then, is several-sided. It can be an expression of the Dharma, an occasion for people coming together to shore up one another's commitment to the Dharma, and a disciplinary way of making one's professions of faith practical, effective. When Buddhist ritual has added aids for the senses, it has taught its people that the Dharma makes an impact on the whole person, not just the mind.

In devotional sects, whose chantings became perhaps the principle focus of their faith, ritual has been even more significant. Nichiren Buddhists, for example, who focus their lives on the *Lotus Sutra,* seeing it in everything necessary for salvation, have become people organized, in their consciousness, around a scripture that assures them of salvation. The message of the Lotus Sutra is that one can be saved through ardent faith alone. It is not necessary to achieve deep wisdom or the quiet of profound meditation. One does not even have to be immaculate ethically. The Buddha is so compassionate, and his Lotus Sutra is so true, that clinging to the Lotus Sutra, believing its message of the Buddha's will-to-save, can suffice. Today one can see American Nichiren Buddhists rise in the morning, come down before a house shrine they have decorated with fruit, candles, and flowers, strike a gong, and chant to the Lotus Sutra in lively faith that relying on it will bring them all good things. That is ritual serving to center a whole life.

WHAT BEHAVIOR DOES GOD REQUIRE?

In Buddhism the question is not so much what behavior God requires as what behavior will lead one to ultimate reality or the divine light that can make one whole. Generally, the Eightfold Path and the five precepts of *sila* outline the behavior incumbent on good Buddhists, but we may delve beneath these to suggest that the key Buddhist behavior is renouncing desire and developing compassion. By renouncing desire the Buddhist strives to snuff out the fires that keep the world burning in pain. By developing compassion he grows like to the Buddha himself, whose compassion for all living things led him to spend the second forty years of his life preaching the Dharma. Cool, serene, peaceful, the Buddha exemplifies desirelessness, freedom from the pains of samsaric existence. Wise, insightful, kindly, the Buddha shows how compassion aids the application of the Teaching to each person's particular circumstances.

Historically, Buddhists often have gotten embroiled in politics and failed to keep the Sangha free of desire for money and power. Historically, they have initiated many charitable reforms but have not always interpreted compassion as practically as an outsider might have hoped. Thus there has not been the passion to minister to suffering bodies, nor to reform structural injustices in society, that there might have been. "Compassion" has tended to focus mainly on the deluded person's spiritual state, inspiring efforts to lead him or her away from karmic entrapments, toward a wiser and more peaceful outlook on things. Concerning desire, the Sangha's fortunes in China, for example, show that at times it prospered from imperial favor, but that at other times it suffered fierce persecutions—the gain and the loss that one experiences when playing tight with the secular powers.

Today Buddhists are making some of their deepest impressions on our global consciousness through their prominence in international movements for peace. During the Vietnam War many Buddhist monks were prominent protesters, some burning themselves to dramatize their spiritual distress. Lately the focus has been opposition to the nations' buildup of nuclear arms, which threatens the survival of the whole planet. In Buddhists' eyes, war of the contemporary types goes directly against the nonviolence, nondestructiveness, and compassion that the Dharma solicits. It is a gross sign of human ignorance, human entrapment in desire. The behavior that the Enlightened One requires is foreswearing these foolish, destructive ways. If, in order to do this, one must also foreswear the desire for money, power, security, or international status that drive the war machines, so much the better. There is no escape from the impact of our desires and deeds, the doctrine of karma teaches, so we had better purify them thoroughly, lest they literally cast the whole world into flames.

The antidote to desire is an intuition of a greater good. If a person can see beyond money, and the tangles to which it leads, she or he may be able to live free of money, make money strictly a matter of means. The same with secular power, the giddy sense of prominent status, and the other things to which we tend to get attached. Sexual pleasure holds many in its snare, so many have to be shown something beyond the joy of sex. Even cynicism is a popular object of desire, many contemporary people enjoying the sharp taste of gloom or hopelessness. Buddhism knows that there are nourishments for the spirit that can make us strong enough to break our bondage to pleasure, status, or cynicism. Therefore Buddhism demands that we grow enough, become mature enough, to take these nourishments and cast our old, debilitating soul-fare away.

If we can do this, and follow the Buddhist program of meditation, wisdom, and morality through to a successful enlightenment, we can become great benefactors of humanity, bodhisattvas filled with compassion. A bodhisattva is a knowledge-being, a person filled with light. This light does not make one arrogant or overbearing. It makes one gentle toward those who still sit in darkness, kindly toward those who are still bruised. Thus Buddhist gurus deal with their pupils tactfully, with a sure sense of what they most need. Pupils differ in their backgrounds and kinds of pain. Where one needs motherly building up, another might need stern goading. But any behavior that the guru exhibits is an effort to extend wisdom and compassion to the given case at hand. Like a wise surgeon, the guru will cut to the quick, if that be the best way to heal. Generally, though, the guru tries to be a model of the serenity and compassion that the pupil hungers after.

When a Buddhist contemplates the translation of desirelessness and compassion from the intimate one-to-one dealings of guru and pupil to the wider social or political stage, complications inevitably arise. Public opinion is a sort of semipermeable shield, often distorting the direct communication that is possible in one-to-one situations. It is difficult, therefore, to speak to the general populace about "desirelessness" and "compassion" without having one's ideas misunderstood. Thus the Buddhist politician likely would take the path of modeling these virtues rather than discoursing on them. In that case one would see in the public arena a leader unconcerned about reelection, above the influence of lobbyists, dedicated in any legislature debate to the deepest and most common good. Behavior of that sort certainly would be striking, outstanding, so much so that it might signal the presence of Buddhist ultimate reality, the Wisdom-That-Has-Gone-Beyond, come into the world of illusion to save many from ignorance.

EIGHT

A Christian View

WHAT DO WE MEAN BY GOD?

Christians mean several things by God: the creator of the world, the Father of Jesus, the Trinity of Father, Son, and Holy Spirit, and Jesus himself in his divine nature. Let us elucidate each of these denotations.

First, God is the creator of the universe, the source of all that exists. When Christian theology found it fashionable to use Aristotelian categories, God was described as the first, Pure Act from whom all the limited beings of space and time derive. As well, God was the universe's final cause, the ultimate good toward which all the processes of the natural and human worlds were directed. In this philosophical scheme, only God was a self-sufficient being. Apart from God's grant of existence, all other beings would collapse back into the nothingness from which God had drawn them. Thus the relation between creatures and God was a participation of the below in the above. Creatures participated in God's being, and so were able to flourish. The very being of any creature, its *is,* was an index of God's creative presence, God's ongoing grant of existence. Thus Augustine could say, "You are more intimate to me than I am to myself."

In the New Testament, however, the conception of God is not derived from Greek philosophy but from Jewish theology. There God is the Adonai or Lord of the Hebrew Bible, somewhat softened and made more intimate by Jesus' use of "Abba." "Abba" means "Daddy." It is the familiar form of "Father." For Jesus, the Lord of creation, the King of the Universe who had condescended to make a covenant with Israel and pledged himself to be with Israel through all its trials, was as approachable and trustworthy as a loving parent. Thus the basic reference of the New Testament's use of God is to Jesus' Father, a personal God making his nature and will known in the flesh of this prophet from Nazareth. In the Johannine writings, Jesus claims that he and the Father are one (John 10:30). The person who sees Jesus sees what human sight can of the paternal Godhead who is Jesus' and every person's source.

As Christian reflection on the relation between Jesus and his Father, and then on the relation between Jesus and the divine force he called the Spirit, matured, the doctrine of the Trinity arose. It is the central Christian mystery (fullness of light too bright for human understanding). There is one God: on this point Christians clung to the Jewish faith of the Shema—"Hear, O Israel: The Lord Our God is One" (Dt. 6:1). But the one God has three "personal" aspects. These aspects do not make for three Gods. They do not make more divinity than the One God alone possesses. Father, Son, and Spirit equally possess the totality of the divine light, love, and life. But they suggest that within the divine reality there are relationships, so that God is a community, a social entity. Without the distinctions or separations that community implies for us human beings, the Father is not the Son but the source, the generator, of the Son. Consequently, the Son is not the Father but the offspring, the one generated by the Father. And the Spirit is neither the Father nor the Son, but the one breathed forth by their love. (Eastern Orthodox Christians attribute the procession of the Spirit to the Father alone, Western Christians attribute it to the joint action of the Father and the Son.)

The Trinity then gives the Christian God three alluring sets of attributes. The Father is the beginning, the unbegotten source, the fathomless background. Like a human memory that is full of all the happenings and thoughts that make a person who he or she is, able to go back and back, the Father is both divinity's and creation's storehouse consciousness (to use a Buddhist figure). Like the light that is the basis of all knowing, divine and human, the Father is the precondition of the Son, the Spirit, and creation. The Son is light from light, a full retrieval of the utter contents of the Father's unlimited memory, a concept completely expressing the comprehensive understanding of the divine mind. When Christians want to emphasize the expression of the Father's life, they speak of God the Son. When they want to emphasize the expression of the Father's mind or understanding, they speak of God the Word. Either way, they believe that the Son expresses the Father completely, so that the two differ only relationally.

The Spirit is the love-force within the Trinity drawing Father and Son into a complete suffusion, a total permeation of one another. Thus some of the early Church fathers spoke of the Spirit as the kiss sealing the love of Father and Son. By the "procession" of the Spirit, the exhalation of the mutual knowing and loving of the Father and the Son, the three "persons" of the Trinity inhere in one another, are thoroughly one.

For mainline Christian faith, Jesus has been the incarnation of the Logos or Word. Thus he has been both human and divine. His resurrection was the main proof for his divinity, but all of his teaching, healing, and goodness pointed in that direction. As the Son incarnate, he naturally was completely oriented to the Father, and naturally was completely filled with, annointed by, the Spirit. Christians find his astounding goodness, to the point of laying down his life for his friends and enemies, the deepest revelation of what God is like: utterly pure, creative, and redemptive love.

WHERE IS GOD IN OUR LIVES?

For Christians, God is everywhere in our lives. Since nothing can exist without God's continuing creation of it, God's ongoing grant of existence, everything points to its divine source. Still, there is a difference among creatures. Natural creatures are vestiges of God, footprints where God walked on the sands of time. Human beings are images of God, due to their reason or spirit. God is in the beauty and power of nature, but human beings reveal something more intimate about the divine nature, its understanding and love. By focusing on human understanding and love, Christian theologians have specified some of the basic qualities of grace, the share in the divine life that God has offered to all people of goodwill.

As a share in God's own life, a communion heart to heart, grace naturally entails knowing and loving. Still, it is a peculiar knowing and loving, one that God himself has both to initiate and receive. In Christian tradition this work is attributed to the Spirit, who is, as it were, God's light and love poured forth in the world in virtue of Jesus' victory. The Spirit is to be for the people who come after Jesus what Jesus himself was for the contemporaries who could experience him in the flesh: another comforter or advocate, one who stands on their side and acts on their behalf.

The Spirit has been thought to do some of her most effective helping and advocacy in the depths of Christian prayer. There, where the believer is open to God in praise and petition, the divine reality at the ground of the human soul moves, as Paul put it, with sighs too deep for words. (Romans 8:26) The knowing and loving of the prayer relationship between the believer and God developed in what some theologians called a "connatural" way. Slowly the person who lived a good moral life and prayed regularly came to think somewhat as God thinks, to love somewhat as God loves. It was like a marriage, in which over the years the spouses come to share many opinions and affections, even seem increasingly to resemble one another physically.

In the mature stretches of prayer, when the person mainly contemplated God's goodness peacefully, there was a growing realization that God is everywhere, does come to us as the inmost reality and implication of every problem, suffering, or joy. In the peak achievements of prayer, when the person became a mystic strictly so-called and felt God's presence directly, the masters spoke of a spiritual marriage, God joining the core of the person to himself like a husband embracing his bride. Thus the knowing and loving that the tradition of Christian prayer has stressed is not abstract or formalistic. It is intimate, person to person, holistic.

God has also been present to many Christians through the Bible. Reading the stories about the Old Testament patriarchs and prophets, contemplating Jesus, or thinking about Paul's advice to the early Christian communities, many believers through the ages felt the strengthening presence of the Spirit, felt drawn again to hope that God would see them through. Bible reading has been a particular love of the Protestant churches, but Roman Catholics and Orthodox also have valued Scripture highly. For them Scripture usually has been read in the context of the liturgy, as we shall explain in the next section, but it has also been a staple of personal piety, especially that of priests and monks.

The sacraments have been another central presence of God. These official acts of the worshiping Church, geared to such times as the birth of a child who was to be welcomed into the community or the Sunday celebration of the Lord's Supper, supplied many Christians the framework in which they understood God's provision for them through the life-cycle: at birth, through maturity, at death. The bread and wine, water and oil, wax and incense of these ceremonies drew all the senses into the worship of God, the response to God's presence, giving depth to the biblical injunctions to taste and see the goodness of the Lord, to take in God's odor of gladness.

Last, many Christians found a special presence of God in the love that arose when two or three, family or friends, gathered in God's name, especially to support one another in time of trial. God was love, the Johannine literature proclaimed. The best analogue for God's nature was the care, interest, healing, enlightenment, power, and self-sacrifice of Jesus' love. When people spent themselves for one another, as parents for children or friends for friends, they brought forward the most godlike parts of themselves. When they came silently to mourn the death of a child or the loss of a parent, they locked arms against the night, the forces assaulting their faith. Many Christians' lives, through history, have been brutally hard, as have most other human beings' lives. The night, when no one could work or believe without fear, was never but a few hours away. So traditional Christians laid the times of suffering and death on the frame of Jesus' passion and death, more or less knowingly. People in the community who were suffering gained a special honor, because the crucifix hung in most sick rooms. At the moment of death, God came to take the person to himself, once and for all. There was no Christian doctrine of reincarnation, no endless cycles of birth and death. The lifeline ran straight from conception to God's judgment, in hope that God would make death a gateway to heaven, his presence for all eternity.

IS THERE A PRIVILEGED WAY TO GOD?

For Catholic and Orthodox Christians, the privileged way to God has been the Sunday liturgy. "Liturgy" means "work of the people." Technically it embraces all of the sacraments (baptism, confirmation, penance, holy orders, marriage, last annointing, and the eucharist), but its main impact in the ordinary believer's life has been the *eucharist* (or divine liturgy, or Lord's Supper, or mass). Essentially, the eucharist ("thanksgiving") is a commemoration or memorial of what the gospels portray Jesus having done with his disciples before his death. The gospels picture Jesus celebrating the *passover* (a Jewish feast in memory of the Exodus from Egypt) and transforming its ritual into a way of being with his people for all time. By making the bread and wine of the passover ritual a mode of his own presence, Jesus assured his followers that he would always be with them, as the food and drink of their spiritual lives. Thus the Catholic and Orthodox churches have found *"communion,"* the consumption of the bread and wine that have been transformed into Jesus' body and blood, a most intense presence of God in their midst. Each Sunday these churches reenact Jesus' last meal, his suffering, death, and resurrection, accepting his invitation to eat of his substance and remember what he did for them.

The eucharistic liturgy also has scriptural and social motifs. In its first part, the priestly celebrants offer prayers and readings largely based on the Old and New Testaments. The purpose of these prayers and readings is to open the people to God, in praise and petition, and to reinsert the people into the story that defines who they are, the story of "salvation history." From the beginnings of God's covenant with Abraham, through to the climax of God's redemptive activity in Christ, Christians understand the biblical story to hammer out a frame on which to stretch all of human time. Taking the Hebrew Bible to themselves, the early Christians read Jesus as the fulfillment of various "types" that the Hebrew Bible had featured. Thus Jesus was the Messiah of whom the prophets had spoken, the new Moses giving a more perfect law, the new David ruling a new Israel. In the New Testament readings of the first portion of the eucharistic liturgy, the people heard stories about Jesus' teachings, healings, miracles, and acts of kindness that brought the Old Testament types to completion. Paul's advice to the early churches gave the people a perspective on their own life and times, while the book of Revelation reminded them of the dazzling power that had burst forth in Jesus' resurrection. Thus the scriptural readings set the stage for the people to rivet again on the central part of Jesus' drama, his passover from death to life, from suffering to resurrection.

The central prayer ("*canon*") commemorating Jesus' Last Supper and passover was the holiest part of the Sunday service. A typical contemporary version of this prayer reads as follows:

> We give thanks to you, O God, for the goodness and love which you have made known to us in creation; in the calling of Israel to be your people; in your Word spoken through the prophets; and above all in the Word made flesh, Jesus, your Son. For in these last days you sent him to be incarnate from the Virgin Mary, to be the Savior and Redeemer of the world. In him, you have delivered us from evil, and made us worthy to stand before you. In him, you have brought us out of error into truth, out of sin into righteousness, out of death into life.
>
> On the night before he died for us, Our Lord Jesus Christ took bread; and when he had given thanks to you, he broke it, and gave it to his disciples, and said, "Take, eat: This is my Body, which is given for you. Do this for the remembrance of me." After supper he took the cup of wine; and when he had given thanks, he gave it to them, and said, "Drink this, all of you: This is my Blood of the new Covenant, which is shed for you and for many for the forgiveness of sins. Whenever you drink it, do this for the remembrance of me." Therefore, according to his command, O Father, we proclaim his death, we proclaim his resurrection, we await his coming in glory.[1]

In this dramatic way, the eucharist brought the past of Jesus' sacrificial actions into the people's present.

For the Protestant churches the privileged way to God was not so much the weekly enactment of the eucharistic ritual as the weekly gathering to hear the Word of God proclaimed again. Thus the Protestant ritual extended the first part of the ancient Christian liturgy ("The Liturgy of the Word"), and made more of the sermon that exposed the scriptural texts. The reading forth of the Bible, and the minister's exposition of what the text had meant in the past and ought to mean in the present, renewed the revelatory, manifestive, proclamatory aspects of the Incarnation of God's Word. Jesus the Word was light for the mind and strength for the soul. To steep the personality again in this font of truth was the central Protestant way of renewing one's contact with God, one's reformation by God.

For all branches of Christendom, the Sunday liturgy was also the prime renewal of the people's sense of the Church, the Christian social body. As branches of Christ their vine, and members of one another, Christians comprised something organic, a single living whole. Their Sunday gathering renewed their sense of fellowship, their bonding in the Lord. Thus the weekly church service was the regular renewal of the community's horizontal connections, its members' ties to one another. It was the community's steady reminder to itself of who it was, what identity God had given it in Christ.

OF WHAT USE IS RELIGIOUS RITUAL?

Prior to the sixteenth-century Protestant Reformation, most Christians did not question the utility of religious rituals. For Luther, Calvin, and the other leading reformers, however, the excesses and aberrations that had crept into the Roman ritual called the Christian ceremonial itself into question. So Protestant Christianity took a step away from the dramatic forms of the traditional eucharistic and sacramental rituals, striving for a more stripped and severe ceremonial pivoted on Scripture. Insofar as hearing Scripture and stirring up one's faith in Jesus' merits were ritualized in the Protestant Sunday service, Christian ritual continued to have a place of honor among the Protestant churches. Insofar as ritual and sacramentalism smacked of perceived "papist" excesses, ritual lay somewhat under a cloud.

The Catholic sacramental system was in effect a series of rites of passage to march the individual through the life-cycle. Baptism (which all the churches agreed was solidly based in Scripture) began the ritual process. Immersed in cleansing water, the infant or the adult convert began a new life in Christ. As Christ went down to death and rose to heavenly life in the resurrection, so the new Christian went down and rose, participating in Christ's passover. The new Christian died to sin and was raised to a new life of holiness, which she or he was expected to treasure, guard, and develop ever after. Sometimes baptism flowed into Confirmation, a sacramental ritual stressing the coming of the Spirit to strengthen the believer for adult responsibilities. Other times Confirmation took place on its own, functioning as a passage into maturity.

Marriage was a further passage into maturity and responsibility, this time for the procreation of life. The Catholic churches considered marriage a sacrament, and used the Pauline symbol of Christ's union with the Church (Ephesians 5:21–33) to deepen believers' appreciation of the holiness of committed sexual love. The Protestant churches did not find a scriptural warrant for considering marriage a sacrament of the rank of baptism or the Lord's Supper, but they usually ritualized marriage impressively. The Eastern Orthodox churches eventually accepted the Roman Catholic scheme of the seven sacraments, stressing that baptism and the eucharist were the most important, and for marriage they developed a royal motif, the bride and groom being like a king and queen sharing a heavenly life.

Orders was the sacrament or ritual through which the churches consecrated their priests and ministers. In the Roman church orders was limited to celibate males. In Orthodoxy the lower clergy could be married but bishops had to be celibate monks (and women could not be ordained). The Protestant churches did not require celibacy and some of them would ordain women. Whatever a church's stipulations, it usually dedicated its clergy in a ceremony that begged for its leadership God's gifts of wisdom, humility, and good counsel. In "high" churches that gave the clergy great power, these ceremonies tended to be full of pomp. In "low" churches that vested most of their power in the community at large, the ceremonies tended to be simpler.

Extreme unction or last annointing was a sacrament or rite for the ill, especially those on the verge of death. Its purpose was to aid both the body and the soul in their time of trial, recalling the merits of Christ and mustering the community's prayers for the sick person's recovery. Funeral rites tended to be ceremonies in the community's regular Sunday style, a eucharistic service among the Catholic and Orthodox churches and a scriptural service among the Protestant.

We have described the eucharist itself sufficiently to indicate how it blended scriptural and sacramental motifs, the main symbolisms of which were Christ's regular feeding of believers' faith and a memorial of Jesus' passover from death to resurrection. The last sacrament in the Catholic-Orthodox scheme was penance, a ritual for the forgiveness of sin. From early Christian times believers had felt the need of ceremonies in which they could confess their wrongdoings, receive advice from church elders, make reparation for the offenses they had committed against God or neighbor, and emerge resolved to sin no more. In the ritual that modern Catholics have called "confession," the believer tells a priest his sins (usually enumerated in terms of the ten commandments), receives an admonition to reform his life, receives assurance of God's forgiveness, and has imposed on him a "penance"—prayers to be said or good deeds to be performed, in reparation for his transgressions. Protestants have tended to favor the private confession of one's wrongdoings directly to God, and Orthodox (especially monks) have had an ideal of completely manifesting one's conscience to one's spiritual director.

Thus Christians by and large have considered rituals to be very useful.

Not making so much of solitary meditation as Buddhism has, the Christian churches have placed before their followers rituals of scriptural or sacramental focus and asked them to believe that these rituals are the main channels of grace, God's own life. To be sure, God could operate outside these regular channels, and private prayer was a fine thing. But the community officially gave first priority to its social ceremonies, especially the eucharistic ceremony in which Christ's own body became the believer's bread of life.

WHAT BEHAVIOR DOES GOD REQUIRE?

The basic moral code for all Christians has been the Ten Commandments, Moses' Decalogue (Exodus 20: 2–17; Deuteronomy 5: 6–21): (1) "I am the Lord your God, you shall not have other gods besides me"; (2) "You shall not take the name of the Lord your God in vain"; (3) "Keep holy the Sabbath day"; (4) "Honor your father and your mother"; (5) "You shall not kill"; (6) "You shall not commit adultery"; (7) "You shall not steal"; (8) "You shall not bear false witness against your neighbor"; (9) "You shall not covet your neighbor's wife"; (10) "You shall not covet your neighbor's goods." All Christians were held to these commandments, as all Buddhists were held to the five precepts of *sila*. The Ten Commandments therefore specified the minimal ethical behavior that Christian faith entailed.

Additionally, good Christians were expected to keep the Church's rules that interpreted or specified the Ten Commandments. Thus when the Church specified a fast for Friday or the days of Lent (a penitential period of forty days prior to Easter, the annual commemoration of Jesus' resurrection), the good Christian was expected to keep it. During many ages of Christian history attendance at the Sunday liturgy was mandatory, while such Church precepts as receiving communion at least once a year, contributing to the support of the Church, and attending the liturgy on special feast days were incumbent on all.

Beneath these precepts of external behavior, however, lay Jesus' own twofold commandment of love. For Jesus himself the essentials of religion boiled down to love of God and love of neighbor. The love of God was to be utter: with whole mind, heart, soul, and strength, as Deuteronomy 6 had specified. The love of neighbor was to be similarly radical: as full as one's love of oneself. For those who got deeply involved with Christian faith and started to appreciate its demands from within, Jesus' command of love became a form of perfection. One could always make further progress in the love of God. There was always a better prayer, a deeper study, a more ardent appreciation that Jesus himself or one of the saints had exemplified. The same with the love of one's neighbor. With the slightest bit of study, it stretched to a wholesale program for better health care, fairer distribution of social resources, a more just political regime, a more peaceful and compassionate approach to domestic or international conflicts. Love was the best human analogue for God, and so love drew all those committed to serious Christianity.[2]

Informally, the different Christian churches placed different emphasis in their moral programs. Roman Catholics developed a church with an almost rigid hierarchial control, so high among the Roman Catholic virtues was obedience to church authorities. Roman Catholics also lay great stress on sexual matters, at least in modern times (the case is less clear for the medieval period), perhaps in part because the celibacy of the clergy made them especially concerned with sexual purity. One sees some remnants of this modern Catholic concern in Rome's strong stands against abortion, contraception, divorce, homosexuality, and the ordination of women.

Protestant virtue came to connote hard work, thrift, and a certain sobriety, especially in the churches derived from the sixteenth-century reformer John Calvin. Joy and high spirits were not the Calvinist style, for the Calvinist view of human nature was rather pessimistic. Only with great discipline could human sinfulness be contained. Among the churches that read the Bible literally, a patriarchal family structure was thought of to be God's will, although the biblical warrant for such further policies as outlawing drinking, smoking, dancing, or card playing is quite obscure. The pious Protestant was directed to the Bible as the source of all good guidance, and in modern times a personal relation with Jesus has been the fulcrum of many Protestants' ethical lives: God has wanted a good friendship with Jesus, a close following of Jesus.

Eastern Orthodox have often interpreted the Ten Commandments rather severely, adding strict rules for fasting and a sober view of death (dressing widows in black, for example). The Orthodox liturgy has counterbalanced this ascetical cast with a great celebration of the divine mysteries, giving Orthodoxy a strong sense of the Spirit's permeation of creation. The divinity of Christ and the holiness of the sacraments have made the liturgy quite solemn, and the striking iconography of many Orthodox churches suggests that the faithful were to contemplate a Jesus, Mary, and body of saints who were quite formal. In Orthodoxy things are not supposed to change quickly, the rule of the fathers of the early centuries being considered quite sufficient for succeeding ages. Thus Orthodoxy has been less modified by modernity and contemporary times than Roman Catholicism or Protestantism, although there are signs that large changes, if not crises, loom on the horizon for Orthodox Christians.

For monks, God has required poverty, chastity, and obedience to a religious superior. For married folk God has required strong devotion to their local church and a generous self-sacrifice on behalf of their children. For single people Christianity has made little special provision, beyond the Ten Commandments and the twofold rule of love. In the final analysis, love has been the epitomizing demand God has made of all Christians, whatever their vocation or church. So Augustine once summarized Christian ethics as, "Love and do what you will."

NINE

An Islamic View

WHAT DO WE MEAN BY GOD?

Muhammad (570–632) meant by God the sovereign Lord of the Worlds. In the Arabia of Muhammad's time, the basic religious instinct was polytheistic. People passed through Muhammad's native city of Mecca not only because it lay on the trade route of the great caravans, but also because it housed the Black Stone (most likely a meteorite) that local Arabs credited with heavenly powers. Soothsayers and diviners did a lively business around the Black Stone, while out in the desert the *jinn* or troublesome spirits held sway. A few of Muhammad's forebears had thought in deeper religious terms, groping after a divinity beyond the polytheistic confusion, but these people never won the popular allegiance. It was only Muhammad's recital of the revelations made to him by Allah, the sole God who made the heavens and the earth, that welded the Arab people into a corps dedicated to the single Lord.

Although there are textual indications in the Koran (the collection of Muhammad's expressions of God's revelations) that Muhammad was influenced by Jewish and Christian views, the wellspring of Islam (the word means "submission") is the prophetic experience of Muhammad himself. Tradition has it that Muhammad grew up as an orphan, and then took over the management of the trading business of a wealthy widow named Khadija. He married Khadija, had children, and seemed set for a prosperous life. But by the time Muhammad was forty he was filled with unrest. So he developed the habit of wandering to nearby caves to find solitude for reflection. Sometimes he would spend the whole night in one of these caves, wrapping his mantle around him to ward off the cold.

Much to Muhammad's surprise, his meditations turned upside down. He began having visions in which a heavenly being spoke to him of the one God and that God's will. Later tradition identified this heavenly being as the angel Gabriel, but Muhammad's initial impression was that he was going crazy. Khadija, however, and others of his family helped him to take the revelations seriously, and before long Muhammad realized that he was being given a heavenly mission. God was telling him to recite (the *Koran* means "recital") or publish the revelations he was receiving, and to reform the Arab people on their basis. Among the major themes of God's revelations were: the divine goodness and power; the need to return to God for judgment, gratitude, and worship (as a response to the divine goodness and power); generosity toward one's fellow human beings; the coming of divine judgment; and Muhammad's own vocation to be the prophet (*rasul*) of God's revelations.

Since the time of Muhammad, God has meant for Muslims the splendid being who seized the prophet and gave him the holy religion of Islam to promulgate. The incomparable nature of this God stands clear in the baseline of the Muslim creed: "There is no God but God, and Muhammad is his prophet." At a stroke, Koranic religion cuts away all polytheism, multiplicity, or confusion about God. The worst sin in the Muslim catalogue is idolatry, setting anything in the place of the sole Lord. Muslims recognize that Jews and Christians had a glimpse of this sole God (although the Christian doctrine of the Trinity sorely compromised Christian monotheism), so they have a special status as "peoples of the book" (their Bible is a forerunner of the Koran). Prophets such as Abraham and Jesus were great religious heroes. But Muhammad is the seal of the prophets, the consummation of the prophetic line, because Allah's revelations to him were the full disclosure of the divine nature and will, never to be superseded.

The effect of this proclamation on Muhammad's contemporaries initially was very slight. A few people in the prophet's household accepted his message, but most of Mecca was unmoved. So the prophet set up in Medina, to the north, and consolidated a following. By 630 he could return to Mecca in military triumph and complete his reformation of the Arab tribes around the transclanic reality of Allah. In the short time between his Meccan triumph and his death (632), Muhammad laid the basis for Islam's amazing rise to Middle Eastern power. His recitals dealt with secular matters as well as matters strictly religious (Islam has never separated the two), so they contained the seeds of a Muslim political program.

The God who had raised up the prophet wanted a people unified around his sole sovereignty. The bloodlines of the clans had allowed too many unfortunates to fall through the cracks: widows, orphans, marginals.

Muhammad made special provision for these people. He improved the status of women, legislated special help for orphans and the sick, and instituted the Islamic alms or tithe, making charity toward the poor a matter of religious obligation. To ensure that people opened up their hearts to the one God, Muhammad legislated praying five times each day, and reciting the basic theological dogma: "There is no God but God." If people would fix their hearts on this sole Lord, rendering him full obedience, they could hope to pass his stern judgment and enter "the Garden," a paradise of flowing streams and shady trees. If they remained in their idolatries and injustices, they would be thrown into "the Fire," the Islamic hell, where they would suffer great punishments. The Lord of the Worlds was compassionate and merciful, but also a stern judge.[1]

WHERE IS GOD IN OUR LIVES?

God is everywhere in our lives. As the creator of the world, he is present to everything that lives and breathes. Human beings he made from humble beginnings, a drop of sperm and a clot of blood, but he is as near to each of us as the pulse at our throats. The splendors of the dawn are Allah's, and the glories of the sunset. He set the moon and the stars in place. The whole natural world testifies to his power. Righteous people, walking his straight path, give evidence of his guidance. Sinners and unbelievers point to his coming judgment, when he will render a verdict on all our struggles with conscience.

However, the house of Islam, as the Muslim community sometimes calls itself, has made the Koran the privileged revelation of God. Muslims are people of the book par excellence, through most of their history considering the Koran to have been directly dictated by Allah. When imagination had had time to play with the implications of this view, Islam came to picture the Koranic text as coeternal with God. (Jews sometimes pictured the Torah similarly.) Thus the Koran stood outside time and was in no way subject to change.

Muslims resisted translating the Koran from Arabic, since that would involve some interpretation of the original pure message. Thus the basic impact of the Koran has come through a passionate, tremulous chanting of the different Arabic *surahs* (chapters), the *Meuzzin*'s (caller's) voice rising and falling poetically. So impressed have Muslims been by the beauty of Koranic Arabic that they have offered this beauty as a proof of the Koran's divine origin: What human being could have produced such a masterpiece? At times the tradition even went so far as to picture Muhammad as having been illiterate, in order further to magnify the wonders of his having recited such splendid poetry.

Since Muslim authority and truth attached in the first place to the Koran, the times when one focused on the Koran were especially apt to reveal God's presence. The Friday service at the mosque was such a time, and so were the times when one studied the Koran with a holy teacher. The basic format of the Friday mosque service was bows and prostrations before Allah, listening to readings from the Koran, and hearing sermons that expounded the text's meaning. People worshiped rather democratically, bowing and prostrating themselves in unison, with little differentiation according to social rank. Women apparently could attend the mosque in early times, but later the segregation of men and women either meant establishing special sections of the mosque for women or virtually closing women out. Since the mosque frequently was a social and cultural center, as well as a place for worship, women's lesser status or exclusion tended to go hand in hand with their being shunted to the margins of the local Muslim society.[2]

Muslim scholarship developed a concentration on interpretations of *Shariah,* Muslim law or "Guidance." Religious students would spend years studying the implications of the Koranic teaching on various points (marriage law, property rights, laws of abstaining from pork and alcohol, and so forth), under the conviction that the divine will for society lay revealed in the Koran and the Muslim tradition. This tradition prominently included the *hadith,* stories about what the Prophet himself had taught, interpreted, or judged in various practical situations that had arisen in Medina or Mecca. The ideal Muslim society was a *theocracy,* a state run by religious law, with no significant separation between the religious and the political establishments. Obedience to the laws of such a society was the ordinary person's best way to fulfill God's will.

For the Sufis, who represent a devotional or mystical stream in Islam that somewhat counterbalanced the lawyers, the divine presence could be experienced through ascetical, meditative, or ceremonial practices (some of which we shall discuss below). The sincere Sufi spurned pomp and position (the name likely means "wool," referring to the simple garb that the original holy men adopted, partly in protest against the luxury that had followed on the early conquests), seeking instead simplicity and quiet in which to pray. The Sufis came to have estimable "brotherhoods," to which lay people could attach themselves, giving material support and receiving religious instruction, and to generate a great number of saints, whose sanctuaries became holy sites filled with the divine presence. Thus the common people often spent much of their religious energy praying at the tombs of deceased holy people, women as well as men, although the style of such veneration greatly varied from culture to culture, that of Morocco, for example, being quite different from that of Indonesia.[3]

The Shiite Muslims of Iran, who represent a divergence from the Sunni majority, sought the divine presence in rather emotional rituals focused on commemorations of Ali, the cousin and son-in-law of Muhammad, whose line the Shiites hold should have determined the descent of the *caliphate* or rulership. The murder of Hasan, the eldest son of Ali, is commemorated as a great tragedy, and the Shiites are similarly emotional in their waiting for the appearance of the Hidden Imam, the leader whom they expect as a sort of messiah. Thus Shiite Islam has made devotional fervor an avenue to the divine, even suggesting that true faith regularly will be impassioned.[4]

IS THERE A PRIVILEGED WAY TO GOD?

Islam has developed a privileged way to God: the "five pillars" on which the faith-structure initiated by the Prophet has come to rest. In considering these five pillars, we look at the basic configuration of most Muslims' faith—the rough equivalent of the Buddhist five precepts and the Christian Ten Commandments.

The first pillar is the confession of faith: There is no God but God, and Muhammad is his prophet. The first surah of the Koran, sometimes called "The Opening," expresses the awesome appreciation of God's sovereignty to which Muhammad's faith had led: "In the name of Allah, the Beneficent, the Mericful. Praise be to Allah, Lord of the Worlds, the Beneficent, the Merciful. Owner of the Day of Judgment, Thee (alone) we worship; Thee (alone) we ask for help. Show us the straight path, the path of those whom Thou has favoured; not (the path) of those who earn Thine anger nor of those who go astray."[5] In their confessions of faith, Muslims try to copy Muhammad's religious awe. "The Opening" has become for many Muslims what the Lord's Prayer is for Christians. It occurs in most Muslim worship, communal or solitary, and many believers do not consider business transactions complete until they have recited The Opening. Probably Muslims have used it in worship since the time of the Prophet himself.

What follows from the confession of faith? In Muslim interpretation, a strict, almost fierce monotheism. As mentioned, the greatest sin in the Muslim catalogue is idolatry: putting anything in the place of the sole God. Only one power runs the Muslim world, and any creature not submissive to this power is in sacrilegious revolt. The great political power of the leaders of an Islamic republic flows from this conception of God. If Allah has granted power to the Caliph or Ayatollah, the Caliph or Ayatollah is powerful indeed.

The second pillar is the injunction to pray five times a day. The purpose of this injunction is to keep the reality of God before the Muslim's consciousness constantly, reminding her or him of the requirements of faith. The five prayer periods ideally pace the Muslim through the day, consecrating all waking hours, from rising to retiring, to the Lord of the Worlds. The Muslim is to make this prayer while facing toward Mecca (in the mosque there usually is a *mihrab,* a niche indicating the direction of Mecca), thereby reorienting him- or herself toward the center of Islamic reality. The ritual prayer involves bowing, kneeling, and touching one's head to the floor in obeisance to God (devout Muslims often develop a bump on their foreheads, which they wear as a proud mark of their piety). If the prayer is being said in common, which Islam encourages, the people coordinate their bows, kneelings, and prostrations, producing a sort of ballet. By the act of prostration the Muslim makes his body an acclamation of Allah's sovereignty.

The third pillar is fasting during the lunar month of Ramadan. Since the lunar calendar moves months around, Ramadan sometimes occurs in the winter, when the days are short, and sometimes occurs in the summer, when the days are long and hot. Regardless, exact Muslims allow nothing to pass their lips while it is daylight. From the time there is light enough to distinguish a black thread from a white, neither food nor drink is to be consumed. Mitigations of this rule have arisen (for example, travelers are not bound), but the ideal is a severe fasting. In the evenings during Ramadan people celebrate joyously, counterbalancing their penances with partying. As with prayer, the bodily discipline of fasting is meant to impress upon the believer both the demands of Allah and the need to muster much will power.

The fourth pillar is almsgiving or *zakat.* By this obligation Muhammad and his successors have sought to bind Muslims together and create a keen sense of brother and sisterhood. The affluent have a duty to look out for the indigent; no Muslim ought to live mindless of the needs of other Muslims. The *zakat* has a scriptural foundation in such Koranic texts as 9:60, and believers often portray it as a loan for which Allah will recompense the giver double. The exact proportions of the Muslim alms have varied:

> *Zakat* is compulsory on monetary wealth, trade goods, livestock, farm produce, and certain other kinds of property, provided a certain minimum quantity is owned. Specific amounts are sometimes a complex matter, but to give an idea, both money and merchandise which have been owned for a full year are taxed at the rate of 2.5 percent. Produce of tilled land is computed at either 5 or 10 percent, depending on irrigation costs. Livestock is taxed in separate categories according to number of head. *Zakat al-Fitr,* the cost of one day's food, is given at the end of Ramadan, the month of fasting.[6]

The fifth pillar is the *hajj* or pilgrimage to Mecca. Every adult Muslim is supposed to perform the hajj at least once during his or her life. The pilgrimage involves ceremonies around the Black Stone, and each year more than a million pilgrims travel to Mecca, the largest number of them during the month set aside for the Great Pilgrimage. The effect of the hajj is to consolidate the house of Islam across nationalities and social classes, since all pilgrims dress in a similar garb and celebrate as strict equals.

OF WHAT USE IS RELIGIOUS RITUAL?

The main use of Muslim religious ritual is to help believers *remember* their dependence on Allah and so live in grateful submission to the divine will. For the majority of Muslims, the five pillars are the strongest training in the virtue of *dhikr* (remembrance), especially the pillars of praying five times each day and fasting during the month of Ramadan. Both of these practices organize the Muslim's time. The five prayer periods organize the day, while the month of Ramadan organizes the year. (For the week there is the Friday holiday, with a special obligation to attend services in the mosque.)

Spatially, turning toward Mecca in prayer and going on pilgrimage to Mecca give Muslims a special geography. The city of the prophet is the center of the Muslim world, the place where the new order initiated by the Koranic revelation was born. After Mecca come Medina and Jerusalem, which are holy sites because the prophet lived in Medina at the beginning of his work and traveled to Jerusalem during his famous "night flight," a visionary experience in which he was rapt up to God. Pilgrimages to Medina and Jerusalem, although not as significant as the *hajj* to Mecca, further help to delineate the Muslim world in terms of the prophet's life and work.

For Sufis the virtue of *dhikr* became all important. In some brotherhoods the ideal was a constant remembrance of God. Different meditative techniques arose to help inculcate *dhikr,* and the Sufis contributed to an impressive Islamic mysticism. At times the Sufi mystics simply pondered the words of a Koranic surah, either letting the words' full significance expand in their consciousness or giving different letters numerical values and so formulating a secret code or set of hidden scriptural meanings. Other Sufi practices included ecstatic ceremonies, such as the dances of the dervishes, through which devotees would become exalted above their ordinary awareness and feel filled with the divine, and a sort of quirky eccentricity, through which Sufis might express their opposition to ordinary society's mediocre religious understanding or practice. This eccentricity was not beyond biting the social hand that had fed it. Thus Hasan of Basra, when asked what Islam was and who were Muslims, replied, "Islam is in the books and Muslims are in the tomb."[7] By this he probably meant that faith was largely a dead letter and the great saints of the past were long forgotten.

Al-Ghazali (1058–1111), probably the greatest of the Muslim thinkers, gave the Sufi disciplines and rituals an unforgettable endorsement when he wrote: "I learnt with certainty that it is above all the mystics who walk on the road of God; their life is the best life, their method the soundest method, their character the purest character; indeed, were the intellect of the intellectuals and the learning of the learned and the scholarship of the scholars, who are versed in the profundities of revealed truth, brought together in the attempt to improve the life and character of the mystics, they would find no way of doing so."[8] For Al-Ghazali, consequently, the Sufi rituals were greatly to be respected.

At the other end of the Muslim psyche from the mystics were the lawyers, who came to dominate Muslim learning. Where the mystics, philosophers, and theologians all seemed to risk creativity, and so to court innovation that might change either Muhammad's vision or the Koranic charter, the lawyers were seen as simply applying Koranic texts, hadith, prior teachings, and the like to contemporary circumstances. To be sure, Muslim legal theory expanded and became an impressive corpus, but almost always it was conservative. For example, in their analyses of human actions the lawyers developed five headings: obligatory, recommended, permitted, disapproved, and forbidden. Thus it was obligatory to confess the unity of God and the prophethood of Muhammad, recommended that one avoid divorce, and forbidden to eat pork. So a rather carefully refined moral code developed, the effect of which was to place the informed Muslim under considerable mental discipline. Insofar as the theories of the different Muslim legal schools came to dominate the different Muslim countries, most of the civil law of the traditional Muslim world ritualized the lawyers' Koran-based prescriptions for individual and social behavior.

So ritual of different kinds, from the Friday service in the mosque to the inculcation of the local legal code, was very important in most Muslims' lives. Discipline was essential to the remembrance of God, and the forgetting of God was the path to perdition. In giving a fictionalized account of the pious upbringing of a contemporary Muslim boy of Senegal, Hamidou Kane has brought home the great beauty and power of the Word that the ritualistically harsh traditional education was meant to magnify:

Once more, trembling and gasping, he repeated the flashing sentence. His eyes were imploring, his voice was fading away, his little body was burning with fever, his heart was beating wildly. This sentence—which he did not understand, for which he was suffering martyrdom—he loved for its mystery and its somber beauty. This Word was not like other words. It was a Word which demanded suffering, it was a Word come from God, it was a miracle, it was as God Himself had uttered it. The teacher was right. The Word which comes from God, must be spoken exactly as it had pleased Him to fashion it. Whoever defaces it deserves to die[9]

In the face of such a Word, no exaction could seem excessive.

WHAT BEHAVIOR DOES GOD REQUIRE?

God requires that the Muslim fulfill the five pillars, live in regular remembrance of the divine goodness and the coming Judgment, and obey the moral precepts of his particular community (which are assumed to be based in the Koran and tradition). The core of this behavior is *submission*: the ready obedience of the creature to the will of the Lordly Creator. Islam is a complete way of life, filling every corner of one's time and imagination. There is no preserve to which God and the Koran are not relevant. There is no time when one may not increase in the purity of one's devotion to Allah or the service of one's brothers and sisters. Devout believers prize the revelations granted to Muhammad as their greatest treasure. The revelations comprise the straight path to the Garden. All other paths court disaster in the Fire.

From the Koran some Muslim regimes have derived a set of behavioral expectations and punishments that have excited astonishment in other parts of the world. Thus the traditional punishment for significant theft has been cutting off a hand, while contact between the sexes that would be considered innocent and casual in many places could occasion a stout whipping. During the Iranian revolution of the Ayatollah Khomeini Muslim tribunals put to death hundreds of the revolution's opponents, showing that the religious power of an ayatollah was nothing to take lightly. Recent Iran is probably an aberration from Muslim history overall, and one could certainly find parallel excesses in regimes driven by other world religions, but it seems safe to say that the recent Islamic fundamentalisms have given the world a disturbingly violent and prudish view of the behavior sanctioned by the Lord of the Worlds.

Traditionally, two points of Muslim behavior have come in for special comment, polygamy and holy war. The Koranic doctrine allows a man up to four wives, assuming that he can support them, and Muslim tradition has permitted rather easy divorce. On the other hand, Muhammad considerably raised the status of women, compared to what it had been in pre-Muslim Arabia, and the Koran legislates some important protections for the wife, the widow, and the orphan, laying the foundation for the rights to inherit and not be abused that the tradition later granted them. Still, traditional Islam is very much a male-directed religion, placing women under strict controls to ensure their modesty. Historically this led to veiling, *purdah* (seclusion from public life), and the harem. In the traditional Muslim's view these developments did not infringe the basic dignity of women, but both outsiders and modernizing Muslims have found them questionable. When coupled with the betrothal of young girls even before puberty, severe restrictions on women's education, and the traditional bias that far fewer women than men make it to the Garden, Islam becomes a big target for feminists. Of course, so do most of the other world religions, East and West.[10]

Holy war or *jihad* has had analogues in Judaism and Christianity, suggesting that prophetic religions regularly submit to the temptation to promote themselves, or the states they inspire, by the sword. By the sword, Islam spread through the Middle East like wildfire after the prophet's death in 632. Within a hundred years it had built an empire that dominated a vast sweep of territory from Spain to the Indus Valley. Holy war only occurred when infidels opposed the rights of Islam to spread, but when the need for combat arose, jihad was a religious duty. One can see "translations" of the original notion of jihad in such modern phenomena as fervent Shiite Iranians flinging themselves into battle against Sunni Iraquis. Part of the Shiites' warrior ideal is the traditional assurance that if they die fighting for Islam they will go directly to the Garden, with its cool streams and buxom maidens.

The golden age of Muslim civilization, however, stretching from perhaps the eighth to the twelfth century, was composed of far more than military conquests. In the golden age the behavior possible to a Muslim, if not required, was wonderfully creative in architecture, poetry, mathematics, and science. Marshall Hodgson's masterwork, *The Venture of Islam*,[11] suggests the full sweep of the Muslim venture. Through his successors' great energy and intelligence, what Muhammad had initiated grew to be the cultural energy controlling the Mediterranean, Northern Africa, the Middle East, southern Europe, and northern India. The presence of nearly 600 million Muslims today, in all parts of the world, would be unthinkable apart from the golden age of Muslim conquest and culture. So at times past the behavior required by Allah has allowed great liberty for creativity and growth. It has permitted the Koranic message to take African and Indonesian garb, to replace such traditional cultures as the Egyptian and the Persian, to win most of Indonesia, parts of the Soviet Union, and enclaves of China.

The reason Islam could be so adaptable and attractive, its promoters say, is the simplicity and depth of its message: One God, One Prophet, all people brothers and sisters, a simple program (the five pillars), no separation of the secular and the religious, a clear division between evildoers headed for the Fire and the devout headed for the Garden. Islam has all that any person requires individually, all that any state requires collectively. For Muslims all good things will come to the family and the world if people will bend their backs, open their hearts, and submit to the compassionate, the merciful. The great requisite is submission.

PART FOUR

The Good Life

W E have considered some representative religions' views of the human quest, evil, and God, trying to sketch the main ingredients of this phenomenon called "religion." Through subquestions under these headings, we have looked at the influence of founders such as Buddha and Jesus, the role that nature tends to play, the sources of social unrest, and the significance of religious rituals. The two central panels of our presentation have been evil and God: the negative force that pushes human beings to find solutions to their painful situation, and the positive force that lures human beings to visions of pure light and love.

As an introduction to these central panels, we considered the human quest, our species' common tendency to conceive time as an adventurous search for meaning and wisdom. To complete our picture of religion as the portion of culture where people have asked the great questions, we now turn to the issue of the good life: How, on the basis of revelation or the collective wisdom of past saints, ought we to live? More exactly, how ought we to regard the primal zones of work, sexual love, prayer, social justice, and ecology? We have anticipated some of these questions, and some of the traditions' responses, in the first three Parts, but in Part Four we consider them more fully, showing the reader three traditions' programs for the good life.

As will soon become apparent, the good life that the religious traditions have proposed is quite different from the good life proposed by the recent materialistic culture of the West. Few of the great religious traditions have placed much stock in material possessions, sensing that moth and worm easily can destroy the fullest of storehouses. No, East and West, the

119

religious traditions have located the core of the good life in such imperishable treasures as learning, wisdom, love, social justice, and harmony with nature. If human beings had sufficient food, clothing, shelter, education, and health care, they were materially blessed. With such material blessings, they could dedicate themselves to the task most in keeping with their specifically human capacities, the task of acquiring a deeper and deeper initiation into wisdom or communion with the gods.

One sees this clearly in the traditional cultures of nonliterate people. For example, the sacred ceremonies of native Australians and Americans that related either to the individual life-cycle or to the annual life of the tribe were portals to the most serious and precious business a human being could undertake: instruction in the mysteries of life and death, of the origin of things and their ultimate destiny. Hunting, gathering, and the other daily tasks of the tribe were not insignificant, but they served the central focus of the tribe on communing with the ultimate powers. Of course, the tribe was always in danger of growing magical, trying to turn the powers of life to its own advantage. But the shamans and medicine men who cared for the tribe's soul regularly resisted this perversion. The sacred was beyond profit and manipulation. The tribe would only have right order and prosperity when it came into harmony with the sacred powers running the world. To try to bend those powers to paltry human advantage was to risk serious misfortune.

In the great cultures of India and East Asia, the good life remained at core a matter of harmonizing oneself with ultimate reality. Thus the Hindu life-cycle sent the aging person back into the forest, to commune with Brahman, while the Chinese "retirement" from busy-ness was an effort finally to harmonize one's life with the cosmic Tao. The variations that Buddhism or Shinto introduced in East Asia merely colored this basic scheme. Buddhist emptiness was as strong an invitation to inwardness as Indian yoga or Chinese Tao, while the Shinto love of nature encouraged the Japanese to make beautiful shrines where one could pacify the soul through reverence of the *kami* or nature deities.

The Western prophetic traditions of Judaism, Christianity, and Islam placed the good life in one's relation to God, the Creator who stood quite apart from the world. Right relation to the Creator would put nature, society, and the self into proper perspective, while wrong relation to the Creator would throw all one's other relations out of kilter. For Judaism and Christianity wrong relation finally was sin, freely chosen moral evil. For Islam it was forgetfulness and weakness, a sign of one's need to resubmit to Allah. Either way, Allah, the Lord of the Worlds, held the key to the good life. All the costly discipline necessary to follow Allah's commands was but small change compared to the riches of Allah's goodwill.

Today the forces of irreligion, such as the Marxist and capitalist materialisms, dispute the values of both the nonliterate cultures and the traditional cultures of China, India, and the Middle East. "Man is the measure," these forces say, rejecting such transhuman standards as Brahman, the Tao, or God. When the religious traditions bury their heads in the sand or oppose modern materialism with a fundamentalist fervor, they seem to prove the irreligionists' thesis that religion is only a throwback to prescientific times, only an atavism born of emotional immaturity. When, however, the religious traditions peacefully exemplify a humanity richer than computers and bombs, they show the modern irreligionists that worshiping technology is but another sign of immaturity.[1] In Part Four we shall never be far from this debate about immaturity, which surely is one of the most crucial of our time.

TEN

A Christian View

HOW OUGHT WE TO WORK?

St. Ignatius Loyola, founder of the Society of Jesus, the religious order that spearheaded the sixteenth-century Roman Catholic response to the Protestant Reformation, believed that we ought to work as if everything depended on God and pray as if everything depended on ourselves.[1] Later commentators, not believing that the saint could have meant what he wrote, changed things around: We ought to pray as if everything depended on God and work as if everything depended on ourselves. One's reaction to these two different versions of the work-prayer relationship reveals quite a bit about one's personal orientation.

Loyala was a mystic, able to find God everywhere. He trained his men to move outside the monastery and a regular religious routine, so that they could serve the Church's needs wherever they arose. Thus Jesuits were theologians at the Council of Trent (1545–1563), missionaries to India, China, and Japan, and the vanguard of a new series of Catholic groups that stressed active service as much as contemplative prayer. For such people, God was in the bustle of activity as well as in the quiet of prayer. The burdens and distractions of work bulked large on the Jesuit horizon, so Ignatius pondered his men's activity deeply. Even though the sixteenth century was not as hectic as our twentieth century, it forced Loyola and others to worry about becoming so busy that they lost their union with God. Part of Loyola's response was to challenge our spontaneous sense of the work relationship. If we narrow our horizons so that what we ourselves do in an enterprise takes center stage, we let ourselves in for debilitating

122

worries and anxieties. If we keep the big picture, in which the agencies of God and other people play major roles, we are more liable to retain our peace.

Certainly the outcome of a work that depends on the dispositions of an outside market or audience largely falls outside our hands. We may make the best house, teach the best class, develop the best healing skills, and still find that our work largely fails, because people don't want quality housing, or won't study what we teach them, or won't follow the theraputic regimes we've laid out. From a Christian point of view, God is the ultimate mover of the market or audience, because only God coordinates the full system of causes that work on people through their genes, their upbringing, their prior education, their thoughts deep in the night. If we surrender this portion of our work to God, acting as though God were indeed the first cause or prime mover, our own responsibilities can come into sharper focus. Our charge is to do what lies within our power as well—efficiently, beautifully, thoughtfully—as we can. Beyond that, we have to let the impact of other people play its part, and let the mystery of God's action remain central. Paul saw this in the case of his own missionary work: "I planted, Apollos watered, but God gave the growth." (I Corinthians 3:6)

So, in Christian perspective, work ought not to be the strained, hypertensive affair we see in many parts of the industrialized world. It ought to be a solid, satisfying imitation of God, the careful Creator of the intricate species of the land and the sea, a solid imitation of Jesus, who was content fully to instruct only the twelve apostles (and willing to bear their constant failure to understand). Work is a mysterious entity in Christian perspective. Economically, it ought to be the sort of social good that E. F. Schumacher expressed in Buddhist terms: primarily a matter of serving the common welfare and the worker's self-expression, not primarily a matter of crass financial profit. Theologically, it ought to be both an expression of the image of God in us, which calls us all to be poets (makers), and a cheerful bearing of our burdens as sinners, people who rightly have to earn their bread by the sweat of their brow.

The other dicta from the Christian or Western tradition that stress the disciplinary nature of human work (such as "Idleness is the Devil's workshop") have their bit of wisdom, but we must constantly balance them with the liturgical wisdom that the most glorious work human beings can perform is offering praise and thanksgiving to God. The business of life, in Christian perspective, is not business. Mercantile work is not an end in itself. To make mercantile work an end in itself is to have lost sight of both God and human beings. (If the work pollutes nature, it is to have lost sight of one's obligations to the rest of creation as well.)

So liberation theologians around the world, Christians concerned with making their faith free people from the various oppressions now grinding them down, have been penning analyses of work, or eloquent outcries, like the following one from a group of Brazilian bishops: "We want a world in which the fruits of labor are shared by everyone. We want a world in which one works not to get rich but to provide everyone with the necessities of life: food, health, a house, education, clothing, shoes, water, and light. We want a world in which money will be at the service of men, and not man at the service of money."[2] For these Christians, we ought so to work that we do not blush before the Creator, who only asks us to love him utterly and our neighbors as ourselves.

WHAT IS GOOD SEXUAL LOVE?

Through much of Christian history, good sexual love has been hard to find. Jesus did not say much about sexual love, mainly accepting the Jewish mores that prevailed in his day (although he did upgrade the status of women, for example by making his stringent ideas about divorce apply to men and women equally). Paul cast much of his ethics in terms of the coming return of Jesus (the *parousia*), and so grudgingly allowed marriage while counseling those who could to remain free. Apparently neither Jesus nor Paul himself married, but both had numerous female friends and disciples. Still, some members of the Pauline school bequeathed the New Testament bits of literature that subsequently have seemed quite misogynistic: "Let a woman learn in silence with all submissiveness. I permit no woman to teach or to have authority over men; she is to keep silent. For Adam was formed first, then Eve; and Adam was not deceived, but the woman was deceived and became a transgressor. Yet woman will be saved through bearing children, if she continues in faith and love and holiness, with modesty." (1 Timothy 2:11–15)

For many of the church fathers, woman was an enigma and a source of temptation. With the rise of Christian monasticism around 300 C.E., sexual continence became the ideal. Thus the men writing most of the ethical rules and hortatory literature often pictured woman as a temptress. Insofar as monastic life became the higher Christian state, and celibacy was extended even to the active clergy in imitation of the monk's supposedly closer union with God, marriage and the equal relation of the sexes stood far down on the list of the Church's pastoral concerns. The Protestant Reformation attacked the monastic life as unbiblical, and elevated marriage to the status of being the normal Christian state, but the Reformers' return to the Bible only brought in a new wave of *patriarchalism,* since both the Hebrew Bible and the Hellenistic culture of the New Testament era treated women as second-class citizens. Thus throughout most of

Christian history there has not been good sexual love in the sense of an (officially supported) easy mutual enjoyment and help flowing between men and women considered to be full equals.

Nor has the Christian ideal for love had much place for romance or eroticism. Generally, Church leaders have considered the mutual satisfaction and delight of spouses in a Christian marriage of secondary importance, the first purpose of marriage being the procreation of children. Indeed, a general suspicion of bodily instincts, in part derived from the Gnostic and Manichean dualisms that infested the Hellenistic culture in which Christianity unfolded, led to placing large brackets around *eros* (the ardent response to beauty), as did the fact that the love which the New Testament most praises (*agape*) is self-sacrificing, even suffering. Some eras of Christian history may have been rather liberal in their interpretation of this constricted tradition (parts of the Middle Ages, for example), and many laity may have disregarded much of what celibate or pietistic clergy said as being out of touch with reality, but the overall tones surely were muted. Through Christian history life has not been for self-indulgence or pleasure-taking. A brief snatch of sensual delight could bring one an eternity of hell-fire.

Somewhat counteracting this repressive side of the Christian psyche were the places in Scripture and tradition where sexual love functioned as an analogy for the divine-human relationship. The Old Testament included passages in Hosea and the Song of Songs that made marriage or erotic love a symbol for the covenant between God and Israel, while the figure in Ephesians that the union between Christ and the Church is like a marital bond implied that sexual love could be utterly holy. The Catholic and Orthodox churches made marriage a sacrament, and the Protestant ceremonial treated marriage with solemn respect, so by implication all the churches' rituals looked upon sexual intercourse positively. Indeed, when they thought about it peacefully, some theologians realized that Christ's full humanity, and the generally sacramental view of reality to which the Incarnation led, meant God's full embrace of matter and humanity, including sex.

Nonetheless, mainline Christianity has been strictly opposed to the exercise of sexual powers outside of marriage. Traditionally, fornication, adultery, homosexuality, and masturbation have all been strongly proscribed. In modern times divorce has become more tolerable, although in many churches it is far from acceptable, but abortion and the rights of women now divide most churches quite deeply. Thus many outsiders have the impression that even today the Christian Church is uneasy with sexuality. Even today good sexual love is hard to find in the theological literature and church manuals (although it may be flourishing in happy Christian marriages and friendships).

Were Christians to attempt an improved theology of sexual love on the basis of the several profoundly positive aspects of their tradition, they might highlight such scriptural dicta as "For freedom Christ has set us free" (Galations 5:1) and "In Christ there is neither male nor female" (Galatians 3:28). For an Incarnational Christian faith, rooted in the Logos' having fully assumed human flesh, sexual love might be as joyous as good eating and drinking, no more to be abused and no more to be feared than any other natural bodily operation. The deep ties to procreation and the mystery of two people becoming one flesh would still cry out for reverence, but without the traditional fear that eros is something unredeemed. Good sexual love for Christians then would be an eros enjoyed in profound faith that Christ has redeemed all parts of our human history and makeup.

WHY SHOULD WE PRAY?

In the Christian view we should pray because prayer is a principal way of loving back the God who has loved us first. Christianity has always sanctioned prayer of petition, in which one asks God for what one needs, but the heart of its theology of prayer has been a praise and thanksgiving offered to God because of the divine goodness. Thus the eucharist takes its name from the act of thanksgiving that should spontaneously well up in the believer's heart when he contemplates the great deeds of God, and the "divine office" that priests and monks have celebrated is replete with psalms praising God. Just as children have every right to approach their parents for help with any of their needs, so Christian believers have felt they have every right to approach God with their petitions. Still, the child who only looked upon her parents as a treasure-trove would be superficial in her love, and so would the purely petitionary Christian.

We should pray, then, as a natural act of gratitude, a natural acknowledgment of God's creative and redemptive presence in our lives. In holding this conviction, Christianity has both continued the archaic traditions' sense that the world is instinct with divinity and referred specifically to the historical teaching and work of Jesus Christ. The archaic traditions saw each sunrise as a marvel, each death something deeply to be pondered. The regularity of sunrises and deaths did not diminish the deep wonder the traditional religions accorded them. For ancient Egypt the sun god crossed the heavens each day in his chariot. For Shinto Japan the goddess Amaterasu was the light and heat that made all things grow. C. G. Jung, the psychologist, found twentieth-century Pueblo Indians still mesmerized by the sun: "As I sat with Ochwiay Biano on the roof, the blazing sun rising higher and higher, he said, pointing to the sun, 'Is not he who moves there our father? How can anyone say differently? How can there be another god. Nothing can be without the sun.' His excitement, which was already perceptible, mounted still higher; he struggled for words, and exclaimed at last, 'What would a man do alone in the mountains. He cannot even build his fire without him.' "[3] In the Roman Empire Mithra, the sun god, had high status. When Christianity made Jesus the *sol justitiae* (sun of justice), fixing Christmas near the winter solstice, when the sun begins to conquer the cold and the dark, it drew on very ancient psychic roots.

We should pray, the Christian also says, as an expression of the life we share with God. The new covenant sealed in the Holy Spirit means a common set of interests between us and God. This is true both for Christians as individuals and for the Christian Church as a whole. The Church expresses this marital or convenantal bonding in its formal liturgy. Year after year, it goes through time, an annual set of festivals, with a God who has promised to be as ongoing experience proves him to be. In other words, the God of the thornbush (Exodus 3:14) is a fellow traveler. Life in relation to this Lord is an ongoing adventure. This is no less true after the decisive fact of Jesus, for Jesus does not remove the mystery of the divine nature but intensifies it. The cruciform pattern of history, in light of Jesus, takes one into the deepest recesses of the divine nature, where God exorcizes freedom that has gone awry by suffering its evil effects in love. Prayer takes us into these deep mysteries, the inmost life of Father, Son, and Spirit. In developed Christian prayer the Spirit moves the petitioner's depths, with sighs too deep for words. So close has the union between believer and God become that God prays to God, the Spirit both speaks and listens.

Another motive for Christian prayer is interceding for one's fellow human beings. In conceiving the Church as the mystical body of Christ, Christianity laid the foundations for its doctrine of the communion of saints—the notion that all Christians, living and dead, comprise a single society. Thus Christians on earth have felt they could pray for friends and relatives in purgatory (a state of purification, prior to entering heaven, that Roman Catholics have emphasized), and Christians in heaven have been thought capable of helping Christians on earth. Thus the saints—those Christians who have exhibited heroic love and been officially recognized as worthy of eternal happiness with God—have been the object of much Christian prayer, especially Mary, the Virgin Mother of God. (Protestantism has downplayed devotion to the saints, mainly because in the sixteenth century it had become rife with superstition, but Roman Catholicism and Eastern Orthodoxy have always approved it.)

In praise and petition, to Christ and the saints, Christians have made prayer the steady nurture of their inner lives. Using the Bible or pious books, they have read the psalms, pondered the gospel stories of Jesus, or moved from the simple pleasures of a fine day to thank their God for the good life he has made:

> A few drops of rain and I feel grateful; the air is so fresh afterwards. I love to sit in the sun. We have the sun so often here, a regular visitor, a friend one can expect to see often and trust. I like to make tea for my husband and me. At midday we take our tea outside and sit on our bench, our backs against the wall of the house. Neither of us wants pillows; I tell my daughters and sons that they are soft—those beach chairs of theirs. Imagine beach chairs here in New Mexico, so far from any ocean! The bench feels strong to us, not uncomfortable. The tea warms us inside, the sun on the outside. I joke with my husband; I say we are part of the house; the adobe gets baked and so do we. For the most part we say nothing, though. It is enough to sit and be part of God's world. We hear the birds talking to each other, and are grateful they come as close to us as they do; all the more reason to keep our tongues still and hold ourselves in one place.[4]

In this way, the prayer of many ordinary Christians has become deeply simplified and contemplative.

HOW CAN WE ACHIEVE SOCIAL JUSTICE?

For Christianity the root of social justice is love of neighbor as oneself. Were human beings to look upon all their fellows as equal in worth to themselves, the great causes of social unrest—disparities in income, racial and sexual prejudice, a self-exalting sense of superiority—would grind to a halt. Social justice is as near and as far as the outlook in which all human beings are radically equal, essentially the same because essentially children of one parent.

On the way to such a fundamental democracy, Christian theology sees the need both to root out the vices that obscure neighborly love and to appreciate the cost of all human beings' redemption. The vices include pride, untoward love of honors, and wrongful desire for riches. The cost culminates in Christ's cross. Because of our desire for riches, many of us ride roughshod over our neighbors, not sharing with them as their equal dignity under God suggests that we should, abusing them, at times even turning them into slaves. Riches usually relate to honors as cause to effect. In most societies the people who grace the headlines and social pages are those with fat bank accounts. But the worst effect of riches and honors is the tinder they give to pride. In fits of pride, prosperous human beings think the world revolves around their little egos. "Were people to know of my worth," they think, "I would constantly be receiving homage." So pride is the root vice that social progress has to extirpate, either by capitalizing on hard times, which devastate much egotism, or by promoting the notion of a Creator God, before whom all members of our species are but dust and ashes.

When they have been laid low, made to taste the truth of their mortality and creatureliness, men and women become liable to the persuasions of true religion. There is little one can do for a person who thinks him- or herself the center of the world, a proud god or goddess, so misfortune can prove a providential blessing, a way back to sanity. Once restored to sanity, however, the person needs to move along to gratitude. The Creator's many blessings (even in time of misfortune) give cause for gratitude, but the astute Christian has found the cross of Jesus the consummate cause. God so loved the world he gave his only Son that the world might find divine life. The cross of Jesus is the price God was willing to pay to demonstrate once and for all the divine goodness and teach for all time the way to overcome human evils. If people were to contemplate one another in the light of Christ's cross, Christianity traditionally has taught, they might begin to see the great value God places on each of his images. From Americans to Zulus, God has considered all human beings worth the blood of his Son, worthy of the lamb that was slain. In traditional Christian piety, the depths of true religion were a gratitude to God that issued in the Johannine logic: "Beloved, if God so loved us, we also ought to love one another" (I John 4:11).

Through most of Christian history, however, good sentiment has not been enough. With increasing clarity, Christian analysts have come to see that justice is not so much a matter of what one feels or says as what one does. The person who says, "Lord, Lord," but does not do God's will cannot expect to be justified. The person who claims to love her sisters but does nothing material to ease their plight is scarcely better than a liar. Social justice is a matter of deeds, structures, and institutions. Important as having the right words and thoughts may be, it is more important to carry them through to the effective production of just economics, education, health care, politics, and the like. Thus today's Christian theologians stress the systematic character of social injustices and call for systemic reforms.

It is not accidental, these theologians say, that we have the current disparities that run along the north-south line among nations, along the racial line between whites and blacks, along the sexual line between men and women. These disparities—in income, educational opportunity, access to political power, and the like—are almost automatic effects of the current social structures. To become serious about achieving social justice—the equal opportunity of all people, the radical egalitarianism that gives all people a fair chance—is to call and work for systematic or structural change. Without such change, most social progress will be rather cosmetic. To be sure, any progress is worth applauding, but one must not be diverted by cosmetics. Until the world values people more than profits, political right more than military might, we all have miles to go before we sleep. The biblical prophets wanted justice to roll down like a mighty stream. The biblical prophets are still waiting.

As individuals, Christian theology says, we can only hope to make limited contributions to social justice, but we must not underestimate the symbolic significance of even limited contributions. If we make our behavior at work, in church, throughout our neighborhood truly just, truly concerned with helping each person get her or his due, the instinctive conviction each person has that justice is what should obtain will get another boost. That may not be enough to keep the dream of justice from fading, so many are the boosts of injustice, but often it will keep hope flickering. So the person who actually gives his neighbor justice, actually loves his neighbor as himself, may be a greater witness than he realizes. To work for social justice, any of us has to keep believing that social justice is possible. Even small achievements become very significant.[5]

HOW CAN WE BE FRIENDS OF THE EARTH?

Ecology has come rather late to most Christian consciousness, but an ecologically sensitive Christian outlook could be as near as a rereading of the Christian doctrine of creation. In the beginning, Genesis 1:1 intones, *God* created the heavens and the earth. Therefore, the Christian theology concludes, the heavens and the earth (and the seas) are not ours to abuse. At most the heavens, the earth, and the seas are the material content of a stewardship that we have received from God. Insofar as the figure of Adam naming the animals (Genesis 2:19–20) symbolizes humanity's central place in evolution, it supports this notion of stewardship. Nothing in the Bible, however, justifies a laissez-faire economy in which human beings would be free to exploit nature as they saw fit. God's giving human beings a commission to subdue the earth (Genesis 1:28) is indeed a writ to develop human creativity, but it is not at all a license to pollute the rest of creation. For Christianity, then, we can be friends of the earth if we let the earth be a fellow creature, a fellow product of God's expressive love. Since the earth derives from God, and not from ourselves, it has the dignity necessary for friendship. The doctrine of creation implies that the earth is not our slave.

A second avenue to friendship with the earth stretches forth in Christian sacramentalism. Insofar as Christian rituals have incorporated bread and wine, water and oil, they have drawn natural creation into the praise of God, the remembrance of God's redemptive deeds. The "sacramentals"—candles, holy water, ashes for the beginning of Lent, and the like—simply extend this principle. As the psalms invite all creatures, great and small, to bless the Lord, so the Christian sacraments orchestrate nature's gifts to the eye, the nose, the mouth into melodies of praise and thanksgiving. Were Westerners but to reflect on the sacramentalism of Christianity, they would be less inclined to pollute the air, foul the waters, acidify the land. These natural basins would not be alien but neighborly, not be inert matter but the stuff of the holiest rites. One does not abuse or desecrate the stuff of the holiest of rites. The environmental destruction in the twentieth century shows that we have lost Christianity's traditional sacramental wisdom.

Third, we can be friends of the earth if we invigorate our imitation of Christ. This phase, "the Imitation of Christ," used to be a staple of Christian spirituality. Thomas à Kempis' book of that title probably has been second only to the Bible in its influence on Christian devotion. Today critical New Testament studies suggest that we know only a modest amount about Jesus' actual words and deeds, and the twenty centuries that separate us from Jesus make it plain that any "imitation" cannot be simpleminded, trying to make a great leap backwards. It is the essential spirit of Jesus—his love of God, his love of neighbor—that current Christians should want to follow, and most Christian theologians remain convinced that the New Testament is a faithful witness to this spirit.

If so, Jesus loved to consider the lilies of the field, the birds of the air, the crops ripe for harvest. He saw nature as an outpouring of his Father's love. If God would clothe in splendor the grass of the field, which is here today and tomorrow thrown onto the fire, what would he not do for human beings? Thus Jesus drew lessons in God's providence from nature's peaceful prospering. The Kingdom of Heaven grew like a mustard tree, from the smallest seed to the mightiest trunk, limbs, and branches. Imitating Jesus, people today could draw similar lessons, finding God in fields and flowers, birds and bears. Nature could again offer perspective, its vast size and vast age smoothing away human anxieties.

Last, to make us friends of the earth, Christianity would have us whittle away the vices that incline us to abuse the earth. These are largely the same vices that incline us to abuse our fellow human beings and thwart social justice: love of riches, love of honors, and pride. There is a proper love of riches and honors, of course, as there is a proper pride, but rather easily those who concentrate on riches, honors, or their own great worth lose their balance and slip into vice. Vice is precisely imbalance, missing the golden mean. Regarding nature, it shows in the very destructive effects of today's industrialization. Certainly our show-case examples of pollution— Love Canal (New York), Cubatao (Brazil), Minamata Bay (Japan)—demonstrate a great abuse of technology. All over the developed world, we have let greed blind us to a great poisoning of the environment. Accidents in nuclear power plants, smog alerts in Los Angeles, a high incidence of black lung among miners, and many other injuries to human beings or the ecosphere force Christian preachers to return to an old message. Neither people nor the environment are to be twisted out of shape for the sake of economic profit. To do so is to commit very gross sins.

The worm spoiling the apple from within is pride, the chief human sin in the traditional Christian catalogue. Fixating on our rights, neglecting our duties and the rights of others (God, nature, fellow human beings), any of us can be an enemy of the earth, a short-sighted and self-serving polluter. Because we do not believe we are creatures, sinners, people destined for the very life of God, we narrow our gaze to what we can grab here and now. Among the lewd this brings the litter of condoms and beer cans. In the boardrooms of power it brings the appropriation of the waters of Georges Bank or Santa Barbara. Either way, Christian faith sees it as enemy action, hateful to the God who made nature beautiful and saw that it was good.

ELEVEN

A Jewish View

HOW OUGHT WE TO WORK?

If we take the traditional view that Abraham is the father of the Jews, Judaism began around 1800 B.C.E. Through such biblical landmarks as the exodus from Egypt, the giving of the covenant law under Moses, the establishment of the Kingdom under David, and the exalted teachings of the biblical prophets, the Jews elaborated the implications of their life as children of Abraham, people chosen by Yahweh, the god of the Hebrews. During the exile in Babylon, when Jews were away from the Temple in Jerusalem, Judaism transferred religious leadership from the priests who had presided over the ritual sacrifices of the Temple to the teachers who interpreted the traditions. After the destruction of the Temple by the Romans in 70 C.E., and the dispersion of the Jewish community, these teachers (rabbis) set about codifying the legal traditions that had arisen, sensing that such traditions would be the people's best defense against disintegration or loss of identity. The fullest compilation of Jewish legal tradition is the *Talmud,* which probably was fairly complete around 500 C.E., so it is in the Talmud that we find most of the traditional notions that have guided the Jewish community. This is true regarding work.

In the talmudic view, work is a duty. A person must not only earn his livelihood but also must contribute to maintaining the social order. The most estimable work was the study of *Torah* (God's Law), so whenever possible men tried to snatch time for such study. Women seldom were allowed to study Torah, but often they both ran the home and directed a little shop or cottage industry, so as to free their husbands to study. Still,

133

for the majority of men some form of secular work usually was necessary, and the Talmud blessed such work: "An excellent thing is the study of the Torah combined with some worldly occupation, for the labour demanded by them both makes sin to be forgotten. All study of the Torah without work must in the end be futile and become the cause of sin."[1] Thus Judaism first says that we ought to work so as to avoid sin—so as to be sufficiently in touch with the real world of nature and human society to reject idleness and keep our feet on the ground.

This striving for balance is characteristic of Judaism, and one of its most winning features. Just as the rabbis never sanctioned celibacy, fearing that it would withdraw people from what was balanced and natural, so they never sanctioned reclusive work, even when it was religious:

> Greater is he who enjoys the fruit of his labour than the fearer of Heaven; for with regard to the fear of Heaven it is written, "Happy is the man that feareth the Lord" (Ps. cxii. 1), but with regard to him who enjoys the fruit of his labour it is written, "When thou eatest the labour of thy hands, happy shalt thou be, and it shall be well with thee" (ibid. cxxviii. 2)— "happy shalt thou be" in this world, "and it shall be well with thee" in the World to Come. It is not written, "and it shall be well with thee," about the fearer of Heaven.[2]

From these two quotations, we catch a glimpse of the rabbis' regular style. To answer a given question or discourse on a given topic, they ransack past tradition, including preeminently the Hebrew Bible, applying past teachings to the topic at hand. Of course such past teachings were voluminous enough to stimulate different interpretations of current issues, but generally the rabbis made a genuine effort to retain the overall outlook of the great teachers of the past and keep to the well-worn convictions. In the case of work, the well-worn conviction was that work is good for the soul, keeps the person well connected with God's creation.

Thus work and the workman had a high dignity. For Jews it was not only necessary that people earn their bread by the sweat of their brows but salutary. Those who were unwilling to work ought not to eat. The tradition divided on the question of the comparable dignity of agricultural and mercantile work. Some rabbis thought that a man without land was not fully a man, while others thought that tilling the soil was the lowest of human occupations. When times were such that agriculture was precarious, or Jews were not allowed to own land, handicrafts understandably became more desirable. One compromise that the rabbis suggested was investing one-third of one's money in land, one-third in business, and keeping one-third liquid.

The Talmud did, however, frown on certain occupations: "A man should not teach his son a trade which brings him into association with women. A man should teach his son a clean and light trade. A man should not teach his son to be an ass-driver, camel-driver, sailor, barber, shepherd, or shopkeeper, because these are thieving occupations."[3] Of course, other rabbis disputed these interpretations, finding most camel-drivers honest or most butchers and physicians wicked. The tanner was disreputable in many eyes (or noses: the smell of his work made it disagreeable), while the perfumer was praised. But perhaps the most despised occupation was that of the usurer or moneylender. A moneylender, in fact, was prohibited from giving evidence in the Jewish courts. In one Talmudic tractate usurers are compared to shedders of blood. One ought not to work in an occupation like usury, because it tears the religious community apart. Apparently Jews were not forbidden to lend money at interest to Gentiles, for throughout the Middle Ages many were money-lenders, both helping the medieval European economy and earning further persecution from the Christian majority, whose leaders connived in the Jews' usury.

WHAT IS GOOD SEXUAL LOVE?

For Judaism, good sexual love, like good work, is that which follows the ordinances of God, keeps one in proper relation to God and one's fellow human beings. In talmudic Judaism the three great treasures of Jewish life are the Torah, marriage, and good deeds, so marriage has been much esteemed. Indeed, according to Jewish legend, God spends much of his time arranging marriages:

> Once a Roman matron asked Rabbi Jose bar Halafta how long it took God to create the world. The rabbi replied that it took six days. The woman then asked, "What has God been doing from then until now?" The rabbi answered, "The Holy One, blessed be He, is occupied in making marriages." The matron scoffed at this, saying that marriage should only take a short time. Indeed, she went home and in one night married off a thousand of her male slaves to a thousand of her female slaves. The next day the slaves came before her, broken, wounded, and bruised. Each slave said, "I do not want the one you gave me." So the woman went back to rabbi Jose bar Halafta and apologized: "I see now that your Torah is beautiful—praiseworthy and true." The rabbi replied, "Yes. God considers making a suitable match as difficult as dividing the Red Sea."[4]

Helped by the local matchmaker, God usually managed to get Jewish brides and grooms together, and the wedding ceremony was a happy occasion for the whole community. Whereas the bride could be expected to come to her husband well prepared to run the household, neither she nor he necessarily was well prepared for conjugal love. As *Life Is with People,* a marvelous source of lore about the Eastern European *shtetl* (village) life that obtained until the Second World War, puts it:

> The popular stereotype of the groom is an innocent who is at a loss despite his academic acquaintance with all the rules in the sacred writings. As a student he has read and reread the minute regulations for connubial behavior but he may need days or weeks in order to suit the act to the written word. The bride is expected to lack even verbal knowledge about this aspect of marriage. The many lectures on wifely duties to which she has been exposed have dealt chiefly with housekeeping, patience, piety, and docility. Very brief formal instruction may be part of the tearful week before her wedding but all that may be left to luck and a husband as unitiated as his wife. If the bride—"it shouldn't happen!"— is menstruating on her wedding night the ceremony is not postponed— "heaven forbid!"—but she is "a bride who is not kosher." Great precautions are taken to make sure that no rule is broken. Until the ceremony of purification has been performed and the bride is "kosher" a little girl sleeps in the bridal chamber, in the same bed with her, an infantile chaperone to protect the newly married pair against the impetuousness of youth.[5]

The menstrual taboo, rooted deep in the biblical past, led to the orthodox Jewish woman's being required to visit the *mikvah* or ritual bath each month. As well, it was one of several factors that led to a general segregation of men from women. Men were supposed to keep their minds lofty and pure for the study of Torah, and women could be a distraction, if not even a carnal temptation:

> The female's voice, hair, and legs are especially bothersome to sages, who cite them as enticements to sexual arousal. There is a tendency to portray women as sexually ardent, even rapacious, so much so that a mythology of female spirits of seduction developed. Along this line one reads, "It is forbidden for a man to sleep alone in the house, and whoever sleeps alone in a house will be seized by Lilith [Adam's wife before Eve, who became a demoness in medieval Jewish mythology]." (Shab. 15b) Excessive conversation with a woman, even one's wife, could cause a man to lose his good memory (a must for talmudic scholarship). Indeed, if a menstruous woman passed between two scholars at the beginning of her period, she would kill one of them; at the end of her period, she would just bring them to strife. Two women sitting facing one another at a crossroads are surely engaged in witchcraft (Pes. 111a). In fact, "The majority of women are inclined to witchcraft" (Sanh. 67a).[6]

Despite these negative images, many Jewish women no doubt became much beloved of their husbands and content in their roles as wives and mothers. The greatest blessing of Jewish sexual love was children, and the union of man and woman became for the Cabbalists, the leading medieval Jewish mystics, an image of the union between Israel and God, or even an image of God's union with the Shekinah, the divine presence. This heritage has stamped even contemporary Jewish family life, making the Jewish home an unusually potent source of religious values and energies. As few other religions, Judaism has revered the production and nurture of children.

The ideal Jewish sexual love was restrained and chaste, in no way an indulgence of the lower appetites. The rabbis were somewhat prudish in their advice about the interaction of the sexes, but conjugal love itself won high praise. One of the customs of the Sabbath was that the spouses would make love (the Sabbath came as God's bride), and wives had the right to conjugal satisfaction from their husbands. However, the three greatest sins in the Jewish moral code were idolatry, murder, and adultery. This led to great watchfulness in matters of sex. "The strictest standard of sexual morality is demanded by the Talmud. That the adulterer is a practical atheist was deduced from the verse, 'The eye also of the adulterer waited for the twilight, saying, "No eye will see me' " (Job xxiv. 15) [Not even the eye of God]."[7] Thus for traditional Jews the only sexual love that could be called good was one that would not blush before the Holy One.

WHY SHOULD WE PRAY?

In the Jewish view we should pray as an expression of our faith that God exists and is willing to befriend his creatures. It is more than legitimate to ask God for what we need, but the higher sense of prayer is communing intimately with one's Creator. This communion is gratifying to the Creator, for it represents the creature at its most grateful and profound: turned back toward the source from whom it derives all that it is. Playing on the similarity between the Hebrew words for prayer and a shovel, the Talmudists asked, "Why is the prayer of the righteous like a shovel?" Their answer was that just as a shovel moves produce from one place to another, so the prayer of the righteous moves God from anger to compassion.

Good prayer must be sincere, coming from a person who deserves to have her or his petition heard. This has meant that one was to do God's will, and not just pray as a prodigal, without any moral preparation. Still, even when a Jew had not been as observant, as well-founded in the fear of the Lord as the Psalms said he should be, he was still to turn to God with his petitions. Indeed, he was to keep on with his petition, never giving up. God might at any moment see fit to grant his prayer, if he showed the divine mercy his steadfastness in faith.

However, Jewish prayer was not just for the individual. Generally, it was more communitarian. Those who had it in their power to pray for the needs of the community at large and failed to do so were sinners, failing in their social obligations. People who did pray for their neighbors were all the more sure of being heard, for this social sensitivity pleased the Lord. Thus most of the prayers uttered in the synagogue were in the plural, not the singular. In the synagogue the overall welfare of the community predominated over the particular needs of individuals. The result was an encouragement of the individual to associate his or her personal needs with the common good.

Certain talmudic texts wax expansive on the great value of prayer, preferring it to sacrifices or good deeds. The example of Moses supported this view: Moses was not heard because of his sacrifices or good deeds but because of his petitions in prayer. When he was beseeching God for a view of the promised land (Deuteronomy 3), God finally answered, "Speak no more to me of this matter." Then God ordered Moses to the top of Pisgah (the slope of the mountains between the Moabite plateau and the Dead Sea). So convinced were the rabbis of the power Moses' prayer must have had, they interpreted this order as God's granting Moses his desire to see the Promised Land.

The ultimate criterion of a good prayer is not what pours forth from a person's lips but what is going forward in a person's heart. A devout person, as it were, takes her heart in her hands and lifts it up to God. Thus portions of scripture (for example, Deuteronomy 11:13) that speak of serving God with all one's heart were interpreted as counsels to sincere prayer. The leaning upon God, reference to God, ardent longing for God, and heartfelt obedience to God that "service" connoted went to the most central part of the personality, the seat of the deepest knowing and feeling.

Naturally prayer from the heart would proceed reverently, mindful of the exalted dignity of the Master of the Universe. In fact, one could say that sincerity and reverence coincided. To dramatize the stance of the sincere petitioner, the Talmud said that one who prayed was to cast his eyes downward but turn his heart up toward heaven. The petitioner was to envision the *Shekinah,* making the divine presence as vivid as possible. This meant not making much noise in prayer. The awareness of God's presence ought to distance the Jew's prayer from that of the pagans, like the devotees of Baal, who "cried aloud. " (I Kings 18:28)

Many talmudic counsels to prayer assumed the context of the synagogue and so amounted to exhortations to support the synagogue services. Thus it was said that if God enters a synagogue and does not find the quorum of ten that prayer requires he is filled with wrath. Anyone who has a synagogue in town and does not enter it is an evil neighbor, while faithful attendance at the synagogue services is a good way to prolong one's life.

We should pray, then, because we have been brought into a covenant with God, blessed be he, and our covenant with God should stamp our whole lives. Prayer is the most direct way of expressing, strengthening, activating our relationship with God. It is the best way to pour out our praise, our hurt, our need. People who do not pray let the coals of their relationship with God grow cold. It is as though they gave their souls no sustenance. By lifting one's heart to the Lord, the soul opens, breathes, receives nourishment. So does the community. Were the synagogue not busy with prayers, the life of the community would atrophy. The main referent of the community would go unacknowledged, and where would Jewish "reality" be?

For traditional Judaism, God was the substance, the rock, of ultimate reality. Not to pray was to wander into dreaming, the neglect of what was most real. That was why the reform movements that came with modernity agitated so many traditional Jews. In deemphasizing the old laws and the old customs of prayer, the reformers seemed to be cutting the cords that had bound the people to the center of reality, the Master of the Universe, for centuries. Not to pray each morning, each midday, each evening was no longer to be a Jew—to make the centuries run dry and end with a whimper.

HOW CAN WE ACHIEVE SOCIAL JUSTICE?

"It has been widely stated that justice is the moral value which singularly characterizes Judaism both conceptually and historically. Historically, the Jewish search for justice begins with biblical statements like 'Justice (Heb. *zedek*), justice shall ye pursue' (Deut. 16:20). On the conceptual side, justice holds a central place in the Jewish world view, and many other basic Jewish concepts revolve around the notion of justice."[8]

For the Hebrew Bible, justice is one of God's primary attributes (Genesis 18:25, Psalm 9:5). The divine commandments, which serve human beings as a framework for their social life, are primarily intended to encourage justice. When human beings follow God's laws, and imitate the way that God acts, they produce justice. In the messianic times, when the annointed leader of Jewish hope will establish a divine regime, all the world will enjoy justice. From justice comes the Torah, and the end or goal of the Torah is nothing but justice.

In God there is little distinction between justice and holiness. Justice also is closely associated with the divine mercy and grace. By talmudic times, in fact, "justice" usually meant works of charity, benefactions wrought not in a legalistic spirit of rendering to each person his exact due but works of love. To the talmudist justice also could connote "truth." "Trust" and "integrity" were further connotations. From justice would come peace and redemption. In justice all the virtues and good effects of holy living gathered as in an epitome. Clearly, therefore, long meditation on God's justice, and on the centrality of justice to the work of achieving a good social existence, made the rabbis pour into *zedek* all the virtues of righteous living.

If we take the Jewish notion of justice as focusing on what human life should be like, we find that justice finally entails the commitment or moral outlook that the Jew ultimately takes on faith. So basic and thoroughgoing is *zedek* that it permeates all human relationships, both institutional and one-to-one. In the case of a Jewish faith sufficient to undergird an entire social outlook, one cannot omit a consideration of God's justice in the sense of theodicy (defending God from the charge that he is the author of evil). Throughout Jewish history, the biblical writers, rabbis, and theologians all wrestled with this problem, and it continues to burn fiercely today, in the aftermath of the Nazi holocaust of six million Jews.

At times Jews entertained the Neoplatonic notion that evil is nothing positive but rather the privation—the lack—of an order or goodness that ought to obtain. At other times they took the view that God permits evil and suffering in order to test the just, with the result that suffering and evil became "afflictions of love." The assumption behind this second hypothesis was that God would more than compensate his people for whatever they had to endure on earth with the incomparable joys of heaven.

Job, the Bible's innocent man suffering for no apparent reason, remains the archetypal human being struggling with the problem of theodicy, and Marvin Pope's estimate of *Job* (the book) is worth quoting:

> Viewed as a whole, the book presents profundities surpassing those that may be found in any of its parts. The issues raised are crucial for all men and the answers attempted are as good as have ever been offered. The hard facts of life cannot be ignored or denied. All worldly hopes vanish in time. The values men cherish, the little gods they worship—family, home, nation, race, sex, wealth, fame—all fade away. The one final reality appears to be the process by which things come into being, exist, and pass away. This Ultimate Force, the Source and End of all things, is inexorable. Against it there is no defense. Any hope a man may put in anything other than this First and Last One is vain. There is nothing else that abides. This is God. He gives and takes away. From Him we come and to Him we return. Confidence in this One is the only value not subject to time."[9]

So, overall, Judaism rests its hopes for social justice on the justice of God. If God is the Creator and fair Judge; if God has given the Torah, which is more than sufficient for human beings' prospering; then obedience to God, studying and following God's law, should bring us social justice. As Jews, we cannot be overly concerned about what the nations do. The nations fall under God's sway just as much as Jews do, and God will see to it that the nations are rewarded and punished as they deserve. The task of Jews is to be a light to the nations, insofar as God gives the people of the covenant certain special insights into the divine nature.

Sojourning with God through time, Jews must grow sensitive to the many ramifications of God's justice. Thus the rabbis spun laws providing for the most painless slaughter of animals possible, the shielding of all members of the community from actions and words that might be shaming, the protection of the stranger who came to live in their midst. Deeper than their sense of prior precedent in these matters was their instinct for what the God of covenant would find fitting, deserving. If the God of Abraham, Isaac, and Jacob had fitted a people to himself for holiness, what behavior should that people manifest, in both its infra-Jewish community life and its life in the Gentile world? It ought to achieve justice by acting justly, compassionately, truthfully, as the Holy One himself had always acted toward Abraham's seed.

HOW CAN WE BE FRIENDS OF THE EARTH?

In Jewish perspective, one of the best paths toward friendship with the earth lies in regaining certain biblical perspectives toward the land. Deuteronomy 8:7–9, for example, beautifully portrays the idealized locale that Israel expected from God: "For the Lord your God is bringing you into a good land, a land of brooks of water, of fountains and springs, flowing forth in valleys and hills, a land of wheat and barley, of vines and fig trees and pomegranates, a land of olive trees and honey, a land in which you will eat bread without scarcity, in which you will lack nothing, a land whose stones are iron, and out of whose hills you can dig copper." The land of the promise was not merely a home, a space the Israelites could call their own. It was beautiful, rich in natural bounties for which the people were to be grateful to God.

After Israel occupied the Promised Land, and grew to the status of a kingdom, various "writing prophets" arose to protest the kingdom's religious failures. Often these prophets' laments mixed the fate of the land with the fate of the people: "For this the earth shall mourn and the heavens above be black; for I have spoken, I have purposed; I have not relented nor will I turn back." (Jeremiah 4:28) "How long will the land mourn, and the grass of every field wither? For the wickedness of those who dwell in it the beasts and the birds are swept away." (Jeremiah 12:4) In the view of a prophet such as Jeremiah, God's covenant embraced the whole natural-human complex, what we today might call the whole "ecology" of Israel's ties with the land. Human beings had not yet separated from nature to the extent that they later would through advanced technology, so what afflicted society afflicted nature, and vice versa.

Claus Westermann, a prominent Old Testament scholar, has reflected on the significance that the biblical psalms still have today:

> In our time the creation psalms again receive important significance, because in the light of science and its results, as well as in our present stance toward nature, the deification of nature has no future (not even if it were to come in the most subtle form of Idealism). There remain only two alternatives: materialism or faith in the Creator. On the one hand, the stars, the atoms, and the earth are seen as only matter. Then we must be understood as coming from matter and consisting of matter. Or else the stars, sun, and earth are related to God just as we are; they are creatures. In that case the ultimate meaning of their living is the same as that of human beings: living to the praise of God's glory.[10]

Nonetheless, despite the Bible's appreciation of the beauty of God's physical creation, and the Bible's association of human beings with other creatures in a single vocation to praise the Lord, Judaism has had some ambivalence about the world. On the one hand, the rabbis, contemplating creation, could agree with the Bible that the world was wonderful, even perfect:

> On this point there was unanimity, *viz.* that the world being the production of God who is perfect must itself be perfect in every respect. Even in the time of its appearance perfection was manifested. On the text, "He hath made every thing beautiful in its time" (Eccles. iii. 11), the remark is made: "In its proper time was the Universe created, and it was not meet for the Universe to have been created before then. Hence one may deduce that the Holy One, blessed be He, created several worlds and destroyed them until He created the present world and said, "This one pleases Me, whereas the others did not" (Gen. R. ix. 2).[11]

On the other hand, no less eminent a contemporary Jewish theologian than Abraham Heschel felt obliged to enter strong caveats about the relation of the world to God:

> The Second Commandment implies more than the prohibition of images; it implies the rejection of all visible symbols for God; not only of

images fashioned by man but also of "any manner of likeness, or any thing that is in heaven above, or that is in the earth beneath, or that is in the water under the earth." The significance of that attitude will become apparent when contrasted with its opposite view. It would be alien to the spirit of the Bible to assert that the world is a symbol of God. In contrast, the symbolists exhort us: "Neither say that thou hast now no symbol of the Godlike. Is not God's universe a symbol of the Godlike; Is not Immensity a Temple?"[12]

Like Christianity and Islam, Judaism has wanted to affirm the goodness of the world, the outpouring of the divine creativity that the natural world represents. Also like them, it has wanted to keep a gap between the world and God, refusing to divinize nature. The problem has come, ecologists now say, from joining the dedivinization of nature with an exaltation of human beings (whom Heschel *would* consider symbols of God)[13] and so making nature something that human beings can use as they see fit. The biblical and traditional Jewish views do not encourage the pollution of nature, but they open the door to such abuse (as do the Christian and Muslim views) by downplaying nature's closeness to God. All three Western traditions might learn something important from the East, where nature's closer identification with the ultimate or divine has provided the basis for a religion of great ecological sensitivity. The Eastern peoples have not fully practiced this religion (they have their own share of ecological sins), but the flowering of their deepest instincts would seem to imply treating nature very reverently, with greater friendship than the West has recognized.

TWELVE

A Buddhist View

HOW OUGHT WE TO WORK?

In an interesting set of exchanges with people who wanted to express their problems with Zen Buddhist philosophy, Roshi (teacher) Philip Kapleau has provided succinct commentaries on many of our modern problems, work high among them. For example, to a questioner who had complained that his company's experiments with meditation had not increased productivity or worker satisfaction, Kapleau replied: "From the Zen standpoint these [the company's experiments] are only stopgap measures, because they deal with the leaves and branches and not with the root cause. They do no more than paper over the gulf separating the worker from his job. So long as managers do not adapt work to the human needs of their workers but insist that workers adjust to the demands of the machine, the laborer will not identify with his work; he will see it as no more than a means to earn money with which to buy more material things for himself and his family, and he will feel alienated. In other words, managers must make work more fulfilling for their workers by involving their workers' hearts and minds and not just their limbs. For their part, workers owe it to themselves to learn how to experience work as a means to personal salvation."

"QUESTIONER: What do you mean by 'salvation'?

"ROSHI: Liberation from the bind of ego, from the deluded notion of a separate reality called 'I.' From the Zen viewpoint, then, work has a far deeper purpose than simply turning out a product or rendering a service useful to society. Rightly regarded, it is a vehicle for Self-realization. But

144

if work is to serve that function, workers must train themselves not to evaluate their jobs as boring or enjoyable, for one can only make such judgments by 'stepping back,' thus separating himself from his work. They must also learn to relate to their jobs single-mindedly, with nothing held back—in other words, with no 'thoughtgaps' between themselves and their work. Performed this way, work acts as a cleanser, flushing away random, irrelevant thoughts, which are as polluting to the mind as physical contaminants are to the body. Thus work becomes an expression of True-mind, creative and energizing. This is the true nobility of labor. To work this way is called in Zen working for oneself."[1]

The Zen position that Kapleau represents depends on the Mahayana philosophical movement toward the identification of nirvana and samsara. In Buddhist schools that stress the difference between nirvana and samsara, there might be greater stress on working in detachment, making sure that one desires neither success nor failure. However, perhaps such detachment is implicit in Kapleau's advice that workers identify with their work and free themselves through work from the bind of ego. Let us meditate on what this might entail.

First, the Buddhist analysis of work, like the Buddhist analysis of many other personal and social problems, instinctively heads for the heart of the matter, the root understanding of reality that the Buddha expressed in terms of the Four Noble Truths and the tradition amplified in terms of the Three Marks. Until a company or an individual gets down to such root matters, their responses are likely to be only stopgap measures, band-aids. The basic problem in work is the separation between the worker and her or his job, what the Marxists have called "alienation." In our time, a principal cause of such alienation is the tendency to fit workers to machines, rather than vice versa. Instead of work being a natural expression of the worker's being, a natural context for the worker's striving for enlightenment, work becomes dehumanizing.

Second, the motive for such dehumanization of work is profit. Both the employer and the worker come to look upon work as simply a means to money and material goods. But, seen as such, work is bound to be extrinsic, alien, held at arm's length. It cannot engage the mind and the heart. So, having to spend a third of their day on something that does not engage them, workers are bound to be unhappy.

Third, Kapleau's advice for solving this problem—overcoming alienation by identifying with one's job single-mindedly—is likely to sound simpleminded and unattractive, at least to contemporary Westerners. If one removes all criticism of work, never judging a task as fulfilling or boring, one removes a major stimulus to make all work more creative. In principle, Kapleau seems to have taken away the basis for attacking the mechanization of human labor: Why not just identify with the machine as it stamps Tab-Tab-Tab-Tab on the bottle caps one is making? Why not abandon the efforts to minimize menial work such as sweeping and washing?

In reply Kapleau might argue that he was stressing what workers should do once they find themselves in a given work situation. At that time (the overall reform of mechanized work having failed or not yet begun), the healthiest approach is to do the work at hand wholeheartedly, whether it be baking cookies, working a jackhammer, or carving exquisite icons. If we refuse to stand back as separate egos but rather involve ourselves completely in our labor, we will unify our mind-body composite and take another step toward the enlightened view that we and all reality are not separate. Thus we will be working as enlightenment suggests we should: as though this time were for the beautiful and useful expression of our connection with all of reality.

WHAT IS GOOD SEXUAL LOVE?

Buddhism has answered the question of good sexual love differently at different times. In the beginning, when Gautama himself stepped forth from the Indian ascetical tradition and sought enlightenment by way of the renunciation of worldly desires, sexual love came under a cloud. The usual expectation was that those wholeheartedly committed to following the Buddha's way would join the Sangha and live in monastic celibacy. Geoffrey Parrinder, in a useful study of sex in the world religions, has developed this point:

> There was criticism of this world-renouncing life, which the Buddha countered in an early dialogue, pointing to the troubles and temptations of family life: "The household life is full of hindrances, a path for the dust of passion. How difficult is it for the man who dwells at home to live the higher life in all its fullness, purity, and perfection. Free as the air is the life of him who has renounced all worldly things."
>
> Therefore the monk, even if he had been a slave before, would be honored by his former master, who would provide him with a lodging place, medicine, robes, and a bowl, and watch and guard him. The monk has put aside all temptations, restrains evil inclinations, masters his faculties, and looks at the inner meaning of all his actions. He is free from the deadly taints of lusts, ignorance, and pain. . . . Buddhism was primarily for monks, and it was said that the monk was the only true Buddhist. There were lay followers from an early date, men and women, but there was no doubt of monkish and male superiority, and lay people who did not join the order in this life could hope to be reborn as monks in the next, though the trials of the monastic life soon appeared.[2]

This point of view is not hard to understand. If desire is the main impediment to enlightenment, and sexual desire is a very strong force, then the renunciation of sexual desire will seem a great blow struck for freedom. The Buddha saw that most people trying to strike this blow would need the support of their peers and the counsel of their elders, so he established the Sangha, the community of people dedicated to the pursuit of enlightenment, the most zealous of whom probably always would be monks. In the monastic environment, from which emanated most of the early writings that interpreted the Buddha's teaching, celibacy was a constant feature, and something of a constant battleground. To gird their loins, monks were apt to lean hard on the aspects of the Buddha's teaching that lent themselves to the exaltation of the celibate life and the soft-pedaling, if not denigrating, of family life. (One can see parallel phenomena in the history of Christian monasticism and celibacy.) Thus the authoritative leaders broadcast the message that the best sexual love was abstinence—transcending sexual impulses for the sake of spiritual freedom.

As Buddhism moved to the East and tried to graft itself upon Chinese and Japanese cultures, however, it found that it had to become more appealing to the layperson. The family or clan was so central to East Asian society that before long Buddhists were speaking of the layperson as capable of enlightenment. Eventually even the Buddhist priesthood (the functionaries responsible for shrine ceremonies) allowed married members.[3] Along with this laicizing movement arose new, usually Mahayana scriptures that exalted married saints such as Vimalakirti, who has been touted as second only to the Buddha in spiritual development:

> The religious orientation and life-style of Vimalakirti made him very popular in China. Being a layman, he illustrated that becoming a monk, with its implied celibacy and childlessness, was not essential for the attainment of enlightenment. His emphasis on religious emptiness recalled Taoist notions of emptiness and detachment. Even the style of Vimalakirti's verbal repartee with his followers was reminiscent of the mode of salon debate fashionable in China in the third and fourth centuries A.D. Both his teaching and his personal demeanor illustrated to the Chinese that Buddhist beliefs and holiness were compatible with their own cultural convictions and heritage. This sutra did not become the exclusive property of any one sect, but enjoyed a broad and continuous influence in Chinese and Japanese Buddhism.[4]

For a tradition such as Zen, which both keeps the monastic ideals of ancient Buddhism and draws upon East Asian cultural traditions, the middle way of the Buddha means affirming that an individual may follow either a celibate or a married path. Still, a contemporary roshi such as Kapleau appears to favor celibacy:

> In the sutras and writings of the masters we find it stated that celibacy—when the body-mind is ripe for it—furnishes the ground for transforming sexual energy into the purer vibrations essential for the deepest states of samadhi and awakening. Celibacy implies much more than abstention from sex. It is a transcendence of sex, a living through and going beyond. This "living through and going beyond" may take a short while or it may require many years. At its highest, celibacy is a rarified state in which the coarse body-mind vibrations have been transformed into the subtlest and finest, producing an all-pervading calm and clarity.[5]

Kapleau goes on to say that one's sexual choice is ultimately a product of one's karma, manifesting itself as what seems best (most conducive to calm religious living) for one's present existence. Overall, then, Buddhism speaks of good sexual love as that which smooths the way to removing desire and so helps one progress toward nirvana.

WHY SHOULD WE PRAY?

Many Buddhist masters likely would respond to this question by saying that it is badly put. In their eyes, we should not pray, if by "prayer" one means addressing a God or god with petitions that stem from one's burning desires. The concept of a God is erroneous, while the many gods that populate the different levels of existence are in the final analysis insignificant for salvation. Desire of any burning sort (apart, perhaps, from the desire for salvation, although even that has to be purified) is a chain to samsara, so desirous prayers of petition, far from advancing the person toward happiness, only prolong his or her imprisonment.

Chogyam Trungpa, the founder of the Naropa Center of Tibetan Buddhism in Boulder, Colorado, has expressed something of the pique that numerous Buddhists apparently have felt over the misinterpretation of Buddhism in the West (and the Western fascination with Zen):

> In the past half century Buddhist ideas have been introduced to Western countries in very impure forms due to the particular viewpoints of the adventurers and translators who interpreted them. It is especially unfortunate that Buddhism has been presented as a theistic religion, whereas in fact it is a nontheistic spiritual philosophy, psychology, and way of life. In recent decades the practice of Zen meditation has become well known in the West. While this is an improvement over the ways in which Buddhism was presented earlier, there is still very little clear presentation

of other forms that meditation practice can take, or of the philosophy which is an essential part of the study of Buddhism.[6]

Trungpa's Tibetan Buddhism has traditionally employed meditation techniques that are more imaginative (more influenced by tantra) than those of Zen, and it is part of the Tibetan Vajrayana tradition to correlate such imaginative meditations with a strongly dialectical study of Buddhist philosophy that emphasizes the emptiness of all things. For Theravada schools, meditation has swung between the Hindu emphasis on trance and the Indian Buddhist emphasis on insight.[7] Either way, the effort has been to purify the meditator's consciousness, so as to improve morality and deepen wisdom. As Kapleau's description of celibacy in the previous section implied a view of the body-mind composite in which the ideal would be to depart from grosser "vibrations" and advance toward purer, so Theravada meditators have tended to think of meditation as purifying the body-mind composite of its more sensual ingredients, that we may become dominated by the higher, more spiritual states of which we are capable. Mahayana meditation has tended to go in several different directions. Ch'an and Zen have exerted a great influence through their practical focus on enlightenment. Whether in the assaulting, vigorous mode of Rinzai Zen, which actively attacks the defenses of nonenlightenment through koans, or in the more peaceful "just-sitting" of Soto Zen, enlightenment, the flooding of the meditator's being with the light that it naturally has, the light that would overwhelm us were we to see ourselves or let ourselves be as we really are (selflessly), is the prime concern. Another group of schools, more philosophically inclined, has put meditation in the service of *prajna*: the intuitive wisdom that sees or understands the world as the Buddha portrayed it to be. The Madhyamika and Yogacara schools, which produced some of the most influential Mahayana philosophy, and such Chinese schools as Hua-yen, likely meditated in this wisdom-oriented way. A third group of Mahayana schools adapted meditation for the laity, in the process opening meditation to devotional or emotional forces and so bringing it closer to theistic prayer.

Thus it is possible, especially within the Mahayana traditions, to find texts and practices that are not nontheistic meditation but rather, for the comparativist scholar trying to place them in the whole spectrum of humanity's religious activities, theistic prayer forms. For example, there are sutras to the Buddha with verses such as the following: "How can there be a likeness to your virtues, untouched by foe or obstacle, everlasting, unlimited, and which cannot be surpassed? There is only one thing that resembles you, O kindly one, the jewel of the Dharma, by gaining which you won preeminence. This form of yours, calm yet lovely, brilliant without dazzling, soft but mighty,—whom would it not entrance?"[8] Similarly, there are expressions of praise to the influential bodhisattva (saint) Avalokitesvara that ring with the fervor of theistic prayer: "Your lustre is spotless and immaculate, your knowledge without darkness, your splendor like the sun, radiant like the blaze of a fire not disturbed by the wind, warming the world you shine splendidly. Eminent in your piety, friendly in your words, one great mass of fine virtues and friendly thoughts, you appease the fire of defilements which burn beings, and you rain down the rain of the deathless Dharma."[9]

Nor did devotional Buddhism lack a mother goddess to whom it could direct its prayerful petitions. In East Asia Kuan-yin, a form of the famous bodhisattva Avalokitesvara, functioned as the main religious resource of the majority of lay Buddhists, while in Tibet the goddess Tara functioned similarly. Thus to Tara many Buddhists prayed: "Goddess of the perfection of wisdom, holy Tara who delights the heart, friend of the drum, perfect Queen of sacred lore who speaks kindly. . . ."[10] Overall, then, a fair summary of the Buddhist view of prayer might run: We should meditate or pray as our minds and hearts incline us, seeking always to contact the forces of enlightenment, the holy powers that can make us whole.

HOW CAN WE ACHIEVE SOCIAL JUSTICE?

Social injustice, in the sense of the different advantages that people have as rich or poor, talented or without skills, comes, in the Buddhist view, from karma. Thus, when King Milinda asked the sage Nagasena why all people are not alike, the sage replied: "Your majesty, why are not trees all alike, but some sour, some salt, some bitter, some pungent, some astringent, some sweet?" "I suppose, *bhante* [an honorific term], because of a difference in the seed." "In exactly the same way, your majesty, it is through a difference in their karma that men are not all alike, but some long-lived and some short-lived, some healthy and some sickly, some handsome and some ugly, some powerful and some weak, some rich and some poor, some of high degree and some of low degree, some wise and some foolish. Moreover, your majesty, The Blessed One has said as follows: 'All beings, O youth, have karma as their portion; they are heirs of their karma; they are sprung from their karma; their karma is their kinsman; their karma is their refuge; karma allots beings to meanness or greatness.' "[11]

The long-range solution to the problem of social injustice, therefore, is to improve the karma of all citizens. If they act nobly in their present lives, they will come into their next human existences better primed to treat one another as equals and share the common goods of society fairly.

Reading the early sutras, which presumably stand closest to the Buddha's own preaching, one does not get the impression that social issues loomed large. Normally the Buddha's addresses take aim at the individual person, trying to convince her or him of the Four Noble Truths and moving her or him to action. Nonetheless, Buddhists have spent twenty-five hundred years trying to ennoble the cultures of various lands, so of course they are well aware of social problems and injustices. Thus Walpola Rahula, in "translating" the Buddha's teaching for our current times, does not neglect social issues, out of the conviction that the Buddha looked at life as a whole: "The Buddha did not take life out of the context of its social and economic background; he looked at it as a whole, in all its social, economic and political aspects. His teachings on ethical, spiritual and philosophical problems are fairly well known. But little is known, particularly in the West, about his teaching on social, economic and political matters. Yet there are numerous discourses dealing with these scattered throughout the ancient Buddhist texts."[12]

In documenting this claim Rahula examines some interesting tiles from the Buddhist mosaic of social ethics: Poverty is the cause of immorality and crime; trying to suppress crime by punishments is futile; far more effective is improving the people's economic condition: giving farmers grain, offering businessmen capital, paying workers adequate wages. When asked what conduces to people's happiness, the Blessed One mentioned four things: skill in one's profession; protecting one's wealth against theft or diminishment; having good friends who help one along the path of virtue; and spending reasonably (neither too much nor too little) so that one lives within one's income. In addition, there are four virtues that conduce to one's happiness in the afterlife: having faith in moral, spiritual, and intellectual values; keeping the five precepts of *sila*; practising charity and not craving wealth; and developing the wisdom that leads to the complete destruction of suffering.

For Rahula, Buddhism is equally explicit about matters of war and peace: "The Buddha was just as clear on politics, on war and peace. It is too well known to be repeated here that Buddhism advocates and preaches nonviolence and peace as its universal message, and does not approve of any kind of violence or destruction of life."[13] Thus Buddhism rejects the notion of a "just war," thinking it but a falsehood coined by those who want to justify their hatred, cruelty, violence, or greed. The ten duties of the king that we mentioned in Chapter 5 are one of the Buddha's several efforts to make practical his view that states flourish or fail to flourish largely because of the quality of their leaders. Buddhist lore has stories of the Buddha himself intervening to prevent disputes among people from erupting into wars, and in the example of King Ashoka, who turned away from violence and became the model of a good Buddhist ruler, we have a concrete indication of the good effects an enlightened political power might bring.

So for Buddhism we can achieve social justice if people turn against the bad effects of their past karma and adopt the program of Gautama. Through its emphasis on self-restraint, nonviolence, and compassion, this program encourages people to root out the vices that make for hatred and gouging. With hatred and gouging removed, people might live together in peace, cooperating for the commonweal. The core of social justice is the equal opportunity to share in the goods that become possible when people live together in peace, cooperation, and mutual considerateness. Take away the desires that enflame people to injustice, frame social life in the precepts of *sila,* and you will make gigantic strides toward the best communal existence one can achieve this side of nirvana.

HOW CAN WE BE FRIENDS OF THE EARTH?

In Buddhist perspective we can be friends of the earth if we recognize our kinship with all fellow creatures and practice *ahimsa* (nonviolence) toward them. The kinship is probably stronger in Buddhism than in the Western religions, because Buddhism less clearly has broken with the cosmological myth, more likely keeps all creatures together in one living organism. While nirvana certainly demonstrates the Buddhist intuition of an ultimate reality transcending the cosmos, the mythical mind that forged much of folk Buddhism kept the distance between human beings and animals rather narrow. In the *Jataka* tales, for example, where Buddhist fancy poured faith into stories about the Enlightened One's previous existences, we find a lush garden of magical transformations, through which the Buddha becomes a fairy, a sprite, a marsh-crow, a peacock, a quail, a lion, and other animals in order to teach a lesson or save a soul. The tales dramatically display the notion of *upaya* (skill in means to save creatures), but they also exhibit the compactness of the Buddhist imagination, in which animal and human lives can easily run together, since they are closely placed on the ladder of reincarnation.

The bodhisattva vow that Mahayana Buddhism popularized took human beings' kinship with all living things to heart, for in it a future Buddha would pledge not to leave the world of samsara, not to enjoy his nirvana, until all living beings had been saved. In the vast stretches of Indian time, this vow could be uttered peacefully, for there was no reason for haste. Behind it, though, was an instinct that all life is connected, so the suffering of one living being stains the happiness of any other.

Ahimsa is a direct expression of this sense of the solidarity of all life, but also an expression of a well-ordered consciousness. That is, Buddhists practice nonviolence both because they value other creatures and because violence is an expression of disordered, karma-inducing motivations. At times this subjective concern for the karmic effects of an action conspires with the objective desire to treat fellow creatures peacefully to produce ethical quandaries that probably appear strange to Western eyes. Winston King has illustrated this sort of quandary with the case of killing a poisonous snake about to strike a small child:

> Should I kill a venomous snake that seems to be in the act of striking a small child, for example, there might be some compensation here [some mitigation of the bad karma that ordinarily accrues to a violent deed]. The snake was killed, to be sure, and this is a sin with evil consequences; but the child's life was saved (presumedly) and that is good. Or at least "good" intentions modify its evil to some extent. Both will register in the future account that Kamma [karma] adds up for me. However, a strict Buddhist may well say that killing the snake is most certainly a sin, while it is *not* so certain in fact that the child would have been killed or might not have been saved by other means. Hence my supposedly good deed is of dubious ethical worth.[14]

To get themselves out of such ethical logjams, practically oriented Buddhists can have recourse to another side of the doctrine of karma: It is the fated destiny of some creatures to be injured or destroyed. Thus Burmese Buddhists with whom Winston King discussed the campaign of the army in 1959 to kill rats, crows, and stray dogs admitted that bad karmic effects undoubtedly would flow from these killings, but they consoled themselves that it probably had been the destiny of the offending animals to run into the army's forces of destruction.

In addition to their sense of all creatures' interconnectedness, and their doctrine of ahimsa, Buddhists have a third traditional basis for friendship with the earth. This is the overlap in the Buddhist world view between nature and divinity. Especially in East Asia, nature has been the privileged locus for divinity (in the sense of the ultimate sacrality, the really-realness, that makes everything be). For example, in the poetry of Saigyo, a twelfth-century Japanese monk, nature appears as much more enlightened than human beings, because nature is what it is, does what it has to do, simply, without the divisions and turmoil that afflict human consciousness.[15]

Japanese gardens, Chinese landscape paintings, and many Japanese haiku express this conviction exquisitely. The gardens set off trees and ponds to perfection. The landscape paintings hang mountain tops in mist, making human figures but tiny pilgrims across an emptiness that nature reveres in silence. The haiku of a master such as the seventeenth-century

Zen poet Basho picture April air stirring willow leaves, a butterfly floating and balancing. This is the atmosphere conducive to wisdom. Given true perspective by nature, the body-mind composite may realize its emptiness, the presence of nirvana here and now. To be joined with nature is to reach the East Asian Buddhist center.

With Taoism, Buddhism offers the West many lessons in the impersonality of divinity, the sacredness of nature. Where the West has its doctrines of creation and sacramentality, the East has its keener sense that the ultimate is silent and striking, like the rugged rock thrusting out into the churning sea, like beautiful cherry blossoms beside a tranquil pond. The hush that nature brings to our turmoil, the invitation to stop pushing or analyzing and commune, is the beckoning finger of the holy. In Buddhist eyes we will only be friends of the earth when we consider the earth holy. So long as we do violence to the earth, polluting and defacing it for profit, we will have only a shriveled notion of the holy.

THIRTEEN

Conclusion

IS THERE A COMMON RELIGIOUS WISDOM?

There is a common religious wisdom: Man is not the measure of reality. For archaic peoples, sacral nature was the measure. Thus the American Indian *Wakantaka* and the Eskimo *Sila* objectified the typical conviction of nonliterate peoples that nature hangs together by a holy force, a numinous power. Harmony with this power was the key to prosperity and disharmony with it was the road to disaster. For the civilizational religion of Egypt, the goddess Maat represented the force that keeps the world in order. The Pharaoh mediated Maat to the people, and were the people to fall out of connection with Maat, nature and society alike might run amok.

The story of Western religious wisdom has two "leaps in being," as Eric Voegelin has called them, that were giant steps on the way to differentiating the divine from the natural. These were the Israelite pneumatic (spiritual) experience of a transcendent God, the Lord of the Covenant, and the Greek noetic (intellectual) experience of the Logos, the divine intelligibility that reached into human intelligence, drawing human intelligence toward an immortalizing communion with the primal Being.

Neither the Israelite prophets nor the Greek philosophers completely realized the implications of their experiences of transcendence, but their successors came to the conclusion that the world has been created by God from nothingness. Thus, for Judaism, Christianity, and Islam, all of which combined Israelite pneumatic experience and Greek noetic experience, although in different ways, neither nature, nor human society, nor the human individual could be the measure of reality. Only God, the creator of all that took up space and endured through time, could be the norm or ultimate referent. The Christian doctrine of the Incarnation concretized this conviction: Jesus showed that only divine life could make human beings fully human.

The Eastern story is less dramatic, less easily punctuated. The great Eastern figures are Confucius and the Buddha, neither of whom completely differentiated divinity from nature. Confucius' main interest was the traditional Way that might make human societies prosper. This Tao was also the directive force of nature, so human societies would prosper through harmony not only with their wisest ancients but also with the force that turned the seasons. Still, Confucius' main impact on East Asian society was ethical: The Confucian mores became the backbone of the East Asian family and political life. Buddha was more metaphysical than Confucius, and more oriented to the individual. Bringing Indian religious history to a dazzling consummation, he removed the barriers keeping the individual from union with the whole of reality. By extinguishing desire, and rooting out the notion of a self, Buddha set the individual in the midst of a moving, fluent reality, teaching much of Asia how to dance. Thenceforth the measure of Eastern religion was nirvana, the blissful state of a being in which the flame of desire has been blown out.

The archaic, Western, and Eastern traditions are all humanistic, beguiled by the beauty that human beings might make, so their insistence that human beings are not the measure of reality does not mean any neurotic self-hatred. To commune with Sila, God, or the Buddha-nature has been the traditional religious person's highest fulfillment. As well, it has been the experience around which the traditional religious societies have tried to organize themselves. In their reliance on their shamans, prophets, and sages, the traditional religious societies have agreed that the peak experiences of the holy folk who most intensely communed with the ultimate should become the people's guiding light.

So the light of the divine or transcendent reality has been the common religious wisdom, and prior to the modern era of Western history few human beings doubted that this light was always available for human direction. No matter how dark or stormy a given human era might be, the divine light was never overcome. For without this light none of the illuminations of human insight, none of the intelligibility of nature, made sense. Unless there were light at the center of being, unless being had an intrinsic *bodhi* nature, the lure of light that human beings felt would be absurd, a cruel and unfounded bit of sport. Whatever the caprices of nature or the blindness of human beings, there was too much sense, too much capacity for orderly growth and creative improvement, to abandon either nature or humanity to surdity or sportiveness. The primal mystery was not how there could be evil or why human beings had to die. The primal mystery was why there was something rather than nothing, how the light could continue to shine.

The traditional religious texts on light are so numerous that one could make a full anthology with little effort. One of the most beautiful texts, however, comes from the Koran, reflecting the Prophet's bedazzlement by Allah: "Allah is the light of the heavens and the earth. The similitude of His light is as a niche wherein is a lamp. The lamp is in a glass. The glass is, as it were, a shining star. (This lamp is) kindled from a blessed tree, an olive neither of the East nor of the West, whose oil would almost glow forth (of itself) though no fire touched it. Light upon light, Allah guideth unto His light whom He will."[1] Commonly, the wise people of the traditional religions have been willing to sell all that they owned to walk in such light. Commonly, they have made such light their rock and their salvation, so they have feared nothing this-worldly.

IS THERE A COMMON RELIGIOUS MEDITATION?

No, there is not a common religious meditation, although archaic shamanism, Western prophetic contemplation, and Eastern yogic concentration bear important similarities. Mircea Eliade's famous monograph on shamanism uses a working definition of "archaic techniques of ecstasy."[2] In Eliade's view, the central religious personage of most nonliterate tribes gained his power (to commune with the gods, heal sick members of the tribe, guide the souls of the dead to their rest, and the like) by going out of himself, leaving his body and traveling in spirit to other realms. By dancing, ingesting tobacco, or depriving his senses in solitude, the shaman left ordinary reality behind and sojourned with the deep powers of life. Since the shamanic mind tended to equate the real with the vividly experienced, these imaginative flights were quite real.

Moreover, often these flights activated exceptional psychic powers, leading to clairvoyance, clairaudience, or an intuition of a client's inmost secrets. The world to which the shaman's ecstasy took him (males tended to predominate in the Siberian shamanism that Eliade made his prototype) was aswarm with powers, both hostile and benevolent. It teemed with ghostly spirits, both animal and human. Fluidly, the shaman would assume the shape of his tutelary animal spirit or become the totem of his tribe. So throughout shamanic interiority, imagination ruled the game. What could be vividly imagined, what came whirling up from the subconscious or blew in when the senses broke from fatigue, dominated the archaic awareness. Often these "somethings" were quite holy, but seldom did reason constrain them to make an orderly whole. Consequently, the archaic thought-world testified to ultimate realities through the principle of the coincidence of opposites. By imagining many options, the shaman pointed beyond every image.

Western contemplation had a greater place for reason. In Judaism the imaginative exercises of the Cabbalists or Hasidim normally were peripheral to the Talmudic piety of the rabbis, which stressed study and a recitative prayer informed by the biblical word. In Islam the mystical forays of the Sufis were perhaps more influential, but once again Law was the mental discipline that prevailed. Christianity took more of Greek *theoria* into its meditative regimes, and Christian monasticism provided a good training ground for mystical prayer. In this mystical prayer, which perhaps represents the peak of the Western meditative regimes, mind and heart rivet on the divine below the level of the imagination and the emotions. According to classical masters such as John of the Cross, the imagination, emotions, mind, and heart all have to be purified, cleansed of their sin and elevated by grace, but the goal of the entire transformation is loving union with God. For all the Western theistic traditions, the light at the core of creation is personal, the effulgence of a creative mind and will. For Christianity the light is the solicitation of love, the overflow of a God not too strange to be believed but too good.

By and large the East did not center its meditative regimes so much on love as on peace. The bhakti sects in Hinduism and Buddhism might qualify this statement, but the yogic experience at the heart of both Hinduism and Indian Buddhism seems eminently to verify it. Thus Eliade's monograph on yoga treats it as ways of acquiring *enstasis* or self-possession.[3] Where the shaman goes out, the yogi goes in, burrowing down to the depths of consciousness, to the ground-level where *samadhi* undercuts all mental content to give a trancelike peace. East Asian Buddhism somewhat transformed this yogic heritage, becoming in Zen, the school most defined by meditation, a holistic effort to unify the body-mind composite and place the individual in the fluid movement of the unified reality that wisdom intuits. Taoists such as Chuang Tzu and Lao Tzu seem to have employed meditative regimes to build up the force of their inner spirits. Riding their imaginations, teasing their minds over paradoxes, opening their souls to the inbreathings of the Great Clod, they became quirky free spirits, at home in an unpredictable world.

In all its forms, meditation, contemplation, or prayer sought to enlarge the practitioner's world, to make her or him deeper and more realistic. Among the strong interiority has never been a flight from realism. It has been the highway to realism. At the juncture of imagination, emotion, mind, and will, the inmost core called the depth of the soul or simply the heart, people the world over have sought, in their different ways, to learn how things configure, what is truly valuable, whence the light emanates. Generally, they have wanted to learn this by feeling it, seeing it, loving it intensely. Generally, the knowledge they have passionately desired has not been speculative but practical, even erotic. Like the knowlege of Adam and Eve, their successful meditations have been acts of intercourse, even conception.

Dealing with the mysteries of life passionately, openheartedly, the religious standard-bearers have come away transformed—impregnated with the Word, flooded with bodhi-light, chastened by Sila's otherness. Still, they have not reported identical methods or experiences. The biblical seers thought that one could not see God and live. The faithful Confucians pondered the Master's "Hear the Way in the Morning, in the evening die content" (Analects 4:8), wondering what the source of such delicious harmony might be. Because they were similarly human, archaic people, Easterners, and Westerners all sought the still point of the turning world. Because they had significantly different cultural formations, they focused on the still point differently: archaic peoples through power, Westerners in terms of an ultimate person to be obeyed or loved, Easterners in terms of what lighted the Way.

IS THERE A COMMON RELIGIOUS MORALITY?

No, there is not a common religious morality, although, once again, deeper analysis finds the traditions agreeing on several central convictions.

Among archaic peoples, morality tended to be what trial and error had shown made for harmony with nature and among the members of the tribe. Thus there was great variety among the mores of American Indians, native Africans, native Australians, and Eskimos. Most tribes feared blood, since it was so close to life, and therefore proscribed homicide, tabooed menstruation, and carefully regulated the killing of game. Similarly, most tribes tabooed death, building fences of custom to ward off its dark powers. Fertility, and consequently sexuality, was a capital force, but something quite transpersonal. Thus fertility ceremonies—for planting, harvesting, marriage, puberty, and birth—were efforts to place both individuals and the tribe as a whole in phase with the fecundity of mother earth, the generative powers of father sky (sun and rain), the feminine periodicity of the moon and the tides. In the hard life that archaic people often faced, courage, strength, and reliability were precious virtues, so often they were inculcated through arduous initiation rites. Thus much of tribal morality was disciplinary, geared to keeping people cooperative and protecting them from the malign portion of nature's many spirits.

Western religious morality has tended to rest on a scripture and develop into a fairly detailed law. For example, both Judaism and Islam developed what they took to be God's Word into "guidance" (Torah, Shariah) for all aspects of daily life. In the process they both lost some of the creative freshness that God's Word had when it burst upon an Isaiah or a Muhammad and saved a good part of that Word's force from the vagaries of human charisma, which may or may not be available to embody the divine Word dramatically. Christianity personalized the divine Word through the Incarnation, making the center of its morality the imitation of the Word become flesh, but Christian dogma also ossified the original revelation, both protecting Jesus' revelation from human caprice and taking away some of its soul.

Whether through law or individual inspiration, the Western religionist has faced a Word of God that demanded obedience. To "hear" the Word has been a euphemism for taking it to heart, acting upon it. The person who said, "Lord, Lord," and did not do what the Lord required was on the slippery slope to the Fire, condemned as a hypocrite as well as a slug. If Muslims have been the most wholehearted submitters, the people most awed by the majesty of the Lord of the Worlds, Christians and Jews also have been bound, summoned to enact a justice and mercy they themselves had not laid out.

Considerble love, however, enters into Jewish and Christian obedience, especially in the example of the most signal saints, for the epitome of all biblical law is the twofold command of utter love of God and love of neighbor as oneself. Informed by such charity, the virtues of prudence, justice, fortitude, and temperance could become warm and flexible. Studying Torah, marrying responsibly, and carrying out many good deeds, the biblical Westerner tried to make life holy, sacramental, worthy of a God who would join himself to scruffy people, would be so good as to love even this time, when so many have hearts of darkness. For Islam, such loving intercourse with God seems to have been limited to a few Sufis. In the Muslim mainstream, awe and reverence predominated over childlike or spousal love.

Eastern morality waved out from insight, and so was cooler than the passionate, willful morality of the Western religions. Removing desire, the yogin or bodhisattva could treat all people calmly, kindly, without agitation. Great compassion was the peak of the Mahayana virtues, but great compassion resonates differently than the Bible's suffering love. In the vast stretches of transmigrational time, great compassion could move leisurely. Chinese *jen* (humaneness) was alike to Buddhist compassion, giving Chinese formalism warmth and spirit, but the Bushido Code that medieval Japan developed, in which loyalty to one's Lord was the greatest of virtues, shows that Confucian mores often were very hierarchical, very much the servant of social stability and the status quo. Behind the Confucian social cohesiveness ran the ancients' Tao, which was connected to the Way of nature, so most of East Asia behaved very traditionally, moved by time-honored models and a strong desire not to disgrace the clan. Morality largely was doing what one's ancestors had done.

Indian society allowed pleasure, wealth, duty, and salvation as legitimate life goals. In ascending order, the good person pursued these four toward either a better future life (reincarnation) or a complete break with samsara. The key to breaking with samsara was renouncing desire, and the preferred ways to break with samsara were yogic meditation, working without attachments, and a passionate love of a deity such as Krishna, Shiva, or Kali. The *dharma* (duty) elaborated in such traditional codes as *Manu* was India's social cement, along with the archaic strivings for fertility and protection against evil forces that dominated the folk cultures of the rural villages.

At core these different traditional religious mores probably agreed that justice was the key operational virtue. If people played their allotted roles, carried their assigned loads, society would at least limp along. Society finally was in the hands of deep powers that had designated all the people's roles, so obedience to custom or law was obedience to the sacred. One never knew whether such obedience would succeed in warding off evil and making life sweet, but the saints and sages said that with practice walking the traditional way became its own reward.

CAN WE BE SAGES AND PROPHETS?

Yes, we can be sages and prophets. In any given era, at any given place, the essentials of sagehood and prophetship are available. These essentials are a human nature that is phototropic—made to turn toward the light—and an ultimate reality that is lightsome. When a phototropic human nature meets a lightsome ultimate reality in a contemplative mode, the gears engage and we move toward sagehood. When a phototropic human nature meets a lightsome God in a practical mode, the gears engage and we move toward prophetship. The sage ponders the drives in himself that move him toward the light (the drives that the classical Greek philosophers summarized as *zetesis*.)[4] Slowly, the sage comes to realize that the initiative in the wisdom-venture comes from the divine light, which draws us to the good of enlightenment. The prophet is seized by the light of transcendent reality and given a commission to proclaim what transcendent reality or truth demands of people here and now. As long as we can seek, speak, and act, we can be sages and prophets.

That is not to say, of course, that the road to peak human development, as the religions conceive it, is broad and easy. As the paucity of manifest saints, sages, and prophets suggest, the road is narrow and difficult. First, there is the heart of sainthood: being honest and loving to a signal, harrowing degree. Like to it is the heart of sagehood (penetrating the wisdom that has gone beyond all cant and easy convention) and the heart of prophethood (being a friend of God and speaking God's truth fearlessly). These are what the Bible calls hearts of flesh, in contrast to our usual hearts of stone.

For us hardheartedness has become an accepted convention, a sign of manliness. As Eastern Orthodox Christian monks have long been taught, however, the religious truth is quite the opposite. Without tears and tender emotions, we can have little intimacy with God:

> Yes, my friend, in our age of unbelief and carnal life we have become cold. Tears are considered a manifestation of pitiful weakness, something to be despised—good, perhaps, for old women, but no one else. On the other hand, a stony indifference and a hardness of heart are regarded as virility, self-possession, sangfroid. But, in truth, such an absence of tenderheartedness is merely a sign of spiritual death. A Byzantine mystic once said that those who go to Holy Communion without tears and a tender heart, and still more those who, celebrating the Holy Liturgy, remain stonily indifferent, all of them eat and drink the Body and the Blood of the Lord unworthily. They are subject to condemnation. Therefore, cultivate tears and tenderness of heart, because only through them can we come to the purification of our thoughts. There is no other way."[5]

As a regime for sagehood and prophetship, one might choose one of the yogic regimes of the East or one of the studious regimes of the West. If both of these seem too exotic, one may compose a humble regime of one's own, utilizing the natural rhythm of experience and reflection.[6] We all have considerable experience, since for each of us sunrise follows sunset. The difference between those who become wise and those who remain dull is not so much their experience as what they make of their experience, whether or not they learn from it. Most of us, the poet T. S. Eliot saw, have the experience but miss the meaning. All of us make mistakes, but the wise among us seldom make the same mistake twice. How can we start to capture the meaning of our experience? What might promote us to the group that seldom makes the same mistake twice? Reflection.

If we discipline ourselves to reflect each night on what has happened during the day, we may leave the novitiate and move into religious adulthood. Simply by examining our consciences each day, we can gradually learn who we are, what patterns are typical of us, under what circumstances we tend to blow up, what sorts of people fascinate our minds or lure our loins. Then, slowly sensing the context of these reflections, the backdrop of our experience, the vector of our desires to understand and love, we can approach the reality of God, the Mystery of all human time. God is the light of the examined life. God is the love of religion. Reflect upon the core of your doings, upon the light and love that might dominate your consciousness, and you will get onto what the Latin Christian tradition called the *via illuminativa,* the way of insight and discipleship.

Good people—saints, sages, prophets—do what they say. In good people, appearance and reality, practice and ideal, tend to coincide. That is why the sage, concerned with truth, and the prophet, concerned with justice, are but two sides of the developed religious (or simply human) personality. As aspirant sage, the person tries to discern what is real, which things are truly beautiful, what living measures up to the best instincts of her or his heart, the best examples of human history. As aspirant prophet, the person tries to enact his or her most sagacious visions, put his theories to the test, call himself and his times to account, place his money, his time, his talent on the line. Is there any of us who cannot seek the truth and try to embody it? However modest our talents, however circumscribed our situations, is any of us necessarily prevented from reflecting on what happens and trying, next time, to do better? If nothing need keep us from this sort of examined, religious life, we all might one day become sages or prophets. All the potential is there. The religions say that trying to actualize this potential produces the most fulfilling sort of human life. How can we tell whether the religions are right? The course is over. That's the final exam.

Notes

INTRODUCTION

1. See Alfred North Whitehead, *Religion in the Making* (New York: Meridian, 1960).
2. See Paul Tillich, *Theology of Culture* (New York: Oxford University Press, 1964).
3. For biblical background see Walter Brueggemann, *The Land* (Philadelphia: Fortress, 1977).
4. A fine survey of Middle Eastern questions is *A Compassionate Peace,* a report prepared by the American Friends Service Committee (New York: Hill & Wang, 1982).
5. John Bowker, *The Sense of God* (Oxford, England: Clarendon Press, 1973).
6. Michael Polanyi, *Personal Knowledge* (New York: Harper & Row, 1964).
7. Bernard Lonergan, *Insight* (New York: Philosophical Library, 1957).
8. See Frederick Streng, *Understanding Religious Life,* 2d ed. (Belmont, Cal.: Wadsworth, 1976).
9. See Robert McAfee Brown, *Theology in a New Key* (Philadelphia: Westminster, 1978).

PART ONE I THE HUMAN QUEST

1. See Mircea Eliade, *A History of Religious Ideas, I: From the Stone Age to the Eleusinian Mysteries* (Chicago: University of Chicago Press, 1978).

CHAPTER ONE I A CHRISTIAN VIEW

1. See Lucas Grollenberg, *Jesus* (Philadelphia: Westminster, 1978).
2. See Hans Küng, *On Being a Christian* (Garden City, N.Y.: Doubleday, 1976).
3. See Alexsandr I. Solzhenitsyn, *East & West* (New York: Harper & Row, 1980).
4. See Ernst Troeltsch, *The Social Teaching of the Christian Churches* (Chicago: University of Chicago Press, 1981).
5. See Claus Westermann, *The Psalms* (Minneapolis: Augsburg, 1980).
6. Eric Voegelin, *Order and History, I* (Baton Rouge: Louisiana State University Press, 1956), p. 99.
7. See Arnold Toynbee, *Mankind and Mother Earth* (New York: Oxford University Press, 1976).

164

CHAPTER TWO | A BUDDHIST VIEW

1. *The Dhammapada,* verses 1 and 2, trans. Juan Mascaro (Baltimore: Penguin, 1973), p. 35.
2. Edward Conze, *Buddhist Scriptures* (Baltimore: Penguin, 1959), p. 40.
3. Henry Clarke Warren, *Buddhism in Translations* (New York: Atheneum, 1973), p. 352.
4. Edward Conze, *Buddhist Wisdom Books* (New York: Harper & Row, 1972), pp. 77–78.
5. Philip Kapleau, *The Three Pillars of Zen* (Boston: Beacon, 1967), p. 207.
6. E. F. Schumacher, *Small Is Beautiful* (New York: Harper & Row, 1973), p. 51.
7. Ibid., p. 54.
8. Herbert V. Guenther, *The Life and Teaching of Naropa* (New York: Oxford University Press, 1971), p. 69.

CHAPTER THREE | A HINDU VIEW

1. *Isa Upanishad,* verses 4–5, in *The Upanishads,* trans. Swami Prabhavananda and Frederick Manchester (New York: Mentor, 1957), p. 27.
2. Bhagavad-Gita, 18:64–66, in *The Bhagavad Gita,* trans. Ann Stanford (New York: Seabury, 1970), pp. 130–131.
3. See Erik Erikson, *Gandhi's Truth* (New York: W. W. Norton, 1969).
4. For the traditional Hindu views of marriage, and most other social institutions, see A. L. Basham, *The Wonder That Was India* (New York: Grove, 1959).
5. *The Laws of Manu,* IX: 329–31, in *A Sourcebook in Indian Philosophy,* ed. S. Radhakrishnan and C. Moore (Princeton, N.J.: Princeton University Press, 1957), p. 188.
6. R.C. Zaehner, *Hinduism* (New York: Oxford University Press, 1966), p. 110.
7. Mircea Eliade, *Yoga* (Princeton. N.J.: Bollingen/Princeton University Press, 1970), p. 3.
8. The *Yogasutra,* II: 29, in *How to Know God: The Yoga Aphorisms of Patanjali,* trans. Swami Prabhavananda and Christopher Isherwood (New York: Mentor, 1969), p. 97.
9. Charles S. J. White, "Mother Guru: Jnanananda of Madras," in *Unspoken Worlds,* ed. N. Falk and R. Gross (San Francisco: Harper & Row, 1980), p. 27.

PART TWO | EVIL

1. Stephen T. Davis, "Introduction," in *Encountering Evil,* ed. Stephen T. Davis (Atlanta: John Knox, 1981), p. 1.
2. Jean M. Auel, *The Clan of the Cave Bear* (New York: Crown, 1980), pp. 1–3.
3. *Tao Te Ching,* 56, in Arthur Waley, *The Way and Its Power* (New York: Grove, 1958), p. 210.

CHAPTER FOUR | A TAOIST VIEW

1. See Holmes Welch, *Taoism: The Parting of the Way* (Boston: Beacon, 1966).
2. *Tao Te Ching,* 5, in Arthur Waley, *The Way and its Power* (New York: Grove, 1958), p. 147.
3. *Chuang Tzu,* 6, in Burton Watson, trans., *Chuang Tzu: Basic Writings* (New York: Columbia University Press, 1964), p. 81.
4. *Chuang Tzu,* 6:1, in Thomas Merton, *The Way of Chuang Tzu* (New York: New Directions, 1965), p. 60.
5. *Tao Te Ching,* 57, in Wing-Tsit Chan, *The Way of Lao Tzu* (Indianapolis: Bobbs-Merrill, 1963), p. 201.
6. *Chuang Tzu,* 32:14, in Merton, op. cit., p. 156.
7. *Tao Te Ching,* 74, in Wing-Tsit Chan, op. cit., p. 230.
8. Peter Goullart, *The Monastery of the Jade Mountain* (London: John Murray, 1961), pp. 86–89. Quoted by Lawrence G. Thompson, *Chinese Religion: An Introduction,* 3d ed. (Belmont, Cal.: Wadsworth, 1979), p. 32.

CHAPTER FIVE | A BUDDHIST VIEW

1. Richard H. Robinson and Willard L. Johnson, *The Buddhist Religion,* Second Edition (Encino, Cal.: Dickenson, 1977), p. 161. See also Philip B. Yampolsky, *The Platform Sutra of the Sixth Patriarch* (New York: Columbia University Press, 1967).
2. Walpola Rahula, *What the Buddha Taught* (New York: Grove, 1974), p. 85.
3. F. E. Reynolds, "Asoka," *Abingdon Dictionary of Living Religions,* ed. Keith Crim (Nashville: Abingdon, 1981), p. 69.
4. T.O. Ling, *A Dictionary of Buddhism* (New York: Scribner's, 1972), pp. 90–91. The S. N. referred to is the *Samyutta Nikaya,* the third of the five collections of discourses that comprise the Pali Canon.
5. Philip Kapleau, *The Wheel of Death* (London: Allen & Unwin, 1972), p. 87.
6. See Edward Conze, *Buddhist Meditation* (New York: Harper & Row, 1969), pp. 100–103.
7. Winston L. King, *In the Hope of Nibbana* (LaSalle, Ill: Open Court, 1964), p. 279.

CHAPTER SIX | A CHRISTIAN VIEW

1. See David and Eileen Springs, eds., *Ecology and Religion in History* (New York: Harper & Row, 1974); John Carmody, *Ecology and Religion: Toward a New Christian Theology of Nature* (Ramsey, N.J.: Paulist, 1983).
2. See José Miranda, *Marx and the Bible* (Maryknoll, N.Y.: Orbis, 1974).
3. See Jacques Guillet et al., *Discernment of Spirits* (Collegeville, Minn.: Liturgical Press, 1970).

PART THREE | GOD

1. See Huston Smith, *Beyond the Post-Modern Mind* (New York: Crossroad, 1982); Denise Lardner Carmody, *The Oldest God* (Nashville: Abingdon, 1981).
2. Wilfred Cantwell Smith, *Toward a World Theology* (Philadelphia: Westminster, 1981), p. 189.

CHAPTER SEVEN | A BUDDHIST VIEW

1. John Bowker, *The Religious Imagination and the Sense of God* (New York: Oxford University Press, 1978), p. 251.
2. Yoshito S. Hakenda, trans., *The Awakening of Faith Attributed to Ashvaghosa* (New York: Columbia University Press, 1967), p. 37.
3. See Shunryu Suzuki, *Zen Mind, Beginner's Mind* (New York: Weatherhill, 1970).
4. See Winston L. King, *Theravada Meditation* (State College, Pa.: Pennsylvania State University Press, 1980).
5. Melford E. Spiro, Buddhism and Society (New York: Harper & Row, 1970).
6. See Frederick J. Streng, *Emptiness* (Nashville: Abingdon, 1967).

CHAPTER EIGHT | A CHRISTIAN VIEW

1. *The Book of Common Prayer* (New York: Seabury, 1977), p. 368.
2. For a study of the Christian essentials in terms of Jesus' twofold command, see John Carmody, *The Heart of the Christian Matter: An Ecumenical Approach* (Nashville: Abingdon, 1983).

CHAPTER NINE | AN ISLAMIC VIEW

1. See W. Montgomery Watt, *Muhammad: Prophet and Statesman* (New York: Oxford University Press, 1974).
2. On contemporary Muslim women, see E. W. Fernca and B. Q. Bezirgan, eds., *Middle Eastern Muslim Women Speak* (Austin: University of Texas Press, 1977).
3. See Clifford Geertz, *Islam Observed* (Chicago: University of Chicago Press, 1971); Martin Lings, *A Sufi Saint of the Twentieth Century*, 2d ed. (Berkeley: University of California Press, 1973).
4. On contemporary Iran (and other Muslim lands), see V. S. Naipaul, *Among the Believers* (New York: Vintage, 1982).
5. Mohammed Marmaduke Pickthall, *The Meaning of the Glorious Koran* (New York: Mentor, 1953), p. 31.
6. F. M. Denny, "Zakat," *Abingdon Dictionary of Living Religions,* ed. Keith Crim (Nashville: Abingdon, 1981), p. 820.
7. Idries Shah, *The Way of the Sufi* (New York: Dutton, 1970), p. 162.
8. W. Montgomery Watt, *The Faith and Practice of al-Ghazali* (London: Allen & Unwin, 1953), p. 57.

9. Hamidou Kane, *Ambiguous Adventure* (New York: Collier, 1969), p. 4.
10. See Denise Lardner Carmody, *Women and World Religions* (Nashville: Abingdon, 1979).
11. Marshall G. S. Hodgson, *The Adventure of Islam,* three vols. (Chicago: University of Chicago Press, 1958 ff.).

PART FOUR | THE GOOD LIFE

1. See Jacques Ellul, *The Technological System* (New York: Continuum, 1980).

CHAPTER TEN | A CHRISTIAN VIEW

1. See the appendix on this dictum in Gaston Fessard, *La Dialectique des Exercises Spirituelles de Saint Ignace de Loyola* (Paris: Aubier, 1956).
2. Phillip E. Berryman, "Latin American Liberation Theology," in *Theology in the Americas,* ed. S. Torres and J. Eagleson (Maryknoll, N.Y.: Orbis, 1976), p. 61.
3. C. G. Jung, *Memories, Dreams, Reflections* (New York: Vintage, 1963), p. 250.
4. Robert Coles, *The Old Ones of New Mexico* (Albuquerque: University of New Mexico Press, 1973), p. 6.
5. On getting children started, see Kathleen and James McGinnis, *Parenting for Peace and Justice* (Maryknoll, N.Y.: Orbis, 1981).

CHAPTER ELEVEN | A JEWISH VIEW

1. Aboth 2:2, in A. Cohen, *Everyman's Talmud* (New York: Schocken, 1975), p. 191.
2. Ber. 8a, in ibid., p. 192.
3. Kid., 4:14, in ibid., p. 195.
4. See Richard Siegel et al., eds., *The Jewish Catalogue* (Philadelphia: Jewish Publication Society, 1973), p. 158.
5. M. Zborowski and E. Herzog, *Life Is with People* (New York: Schocken, 1962), p. 285.
6. Denise Lardner Carmody, *Women & World Religions* (Nashville: Abingdon, 1979), pp. 104–105.
7. A Cohen, *Everyman's Talmud,* pp. 97–98.
8. Steven S. Schwarschild, "Justice," in *Jewish Values,* ed. Geoffrey Wigoder (Jerusalem: Keter, 1974), p. 194.
9. Marvin H. Pope, *The Anchor Bible Job* (Garden City, N.Y.: Doubleday, 1965), p. lxxvii.
10. Claus Westermann, *The Psalms* (Minneapolis: Augsburg, 1980), pp. 98–99.
11. A Cohen, *Everyman's Talmud,* p. 38.
12. Abraham J. Heschel, *Man's Quest for God* (New York: Scribner's, 1954), p. 120. The symbolist quotation is from Thomas Carlyle, *Sartor Resartus,* III:7.
13. "And yet there is something in the world that the Bible does regard as a symbol of God. It is not a temple nor a tree, it is not a statue nor a star. This symbol of God is *man, every man.*" Ibid., p. 124.

CHAPTER TWELVE | A BUDDHIST VIEW

1. Philip Kapleau, *Zen: Dawn in the West* (New York: Doubleday, 1980), p. 12.
2. Geoffrey Parrinder, *Sex in the World's Religions* (New York: Oxford University Press, 1980), pp. 43–44. The text that Parrinder quotes is from the Digha Nikaya, 1:62 ff.
3. See, for example, Francis Cook, "Japanese Innovations to Buddhism," in *Buddhism: A Modern Perspective*, ed. Charles S. Prebish (University Park, Pa.: Pennsylvania State University Press, 1975), pp. 229–233.
4. J. D. Whitehead, "Vimalakirti," *Abingdon Dictionary of Living Religions*, ed. Keith Crim (Nashville: Abingdon, 1981), p. 795.
5. Philip Kapleau, *Zen: Dawn in the West*, pp. 77–78.
6. Chogyam Trungpa, "Foreword," in *Buddhism: A Modern Perspective*, p. ix.
7. See Winston L. King, *Theravada Meditation* (University Park, Pa.: Pennsylvania State University Press, 1980); Nyanaponika Thera, *The Heart of Buddhist Meditation* (London: Rider, 1962).
8. Matrceta Satapancasatkastrota, Ill: 34, 40; V:52, in *Buddhist Texts Through the Ages*, ed. Edward Conze, et al. (New York: Harper & Row, 1964), p. 191.
9. Saddharmapundarika, XXIV: 21–22, in ibid., p. 195.
10. Aryatarabhattarikanamashtottarasatakastotra, v. 33, in ibid., p. 199.
11. Henry Clarke Warren, *Buddhism in Translations* (New York: Atheneum, 1962), p. 215.
12. Walpola Rahula, *What the Buddha Taught*, rev. ed. (New York: Grove, 1974), p. 81.
13. Ibid., p. 84.
14. Winston L. King, *In the Hope of Nibbana* (LaSalle, Ind.: Open Court, 1964), p. 136.
15. See William LaFleur, "Saigyo and the Buddhist Value of Nature," *History of Religions*, 13 (1973–74), 93–128, 227–248.

CONCLUSION

1. Koran 24:35, in *The Meaning of the Glorious Koran*, trans. Mohammed Marmaduke Pickthall (New York: Mentor, 1953), p. 256.
2. Mircea Eliade, *Shamanism: Archaic Techniques of Ecstacy* (Princeton, N.J.: Princeton University Press/Bollingen, 1972).
3. Mircea Eliade, *Yoga: Immortality and Freedom* (Princeton, N.J.: Princeton University Press/Bollingen, 1970).
4. See Eric Voegelin, "Reason: The Classic Experience," in his *Anamnesis* (Notre Dame, Ind.: University of Notre Dame Press, 1978), pp. 89–115.
5. Sergius Bolshakoff and M. Basil Pennington, *In Search of True Wisdom* (Garden City, N.J.: Doubleday, 1979), pp. 60–61.
6. See John Carmody, *Re-Examining Conscience* (New York: Seabury, 1982).

Time Line

100,000 years ago	Homo sapiens; ritual burial
30,000 years ago	Prehistoric painting and sculpture; Mongoloid peoples cross Bering Strait
8,000-6,000 B.C.E.	Agriculture, domestication of animals, rise of towns
3100	Unification of Egypt; Invention of writing in Sumer
2750	Growth of civilization in Indus Valley
1600	Shang Bronze Culture in China
1500	Vedas, Rise of Iranian-speaking peoples
1200	Exodus of Hebrews from Egypt
800-400	Upanishads
750-550	Hebrew Prophets
ca. 628-551	Zoroaster, Iranian Prophet
599-527	Mahavira, founder of Jainism
551-479	Confucius
536-476	Buddha
500-200	Mahabharata, Ramayana, Bhagavad Gita
427-347	Plato
350	Tao Te Ching
273-236	Asoka
200	Rise of religious Taoism
80	Buddhist decline in India
50	Formation of Buddhist collection of scriptures
30 C.E.	Death of Jesus of Nazareth
50-95	New Testament writings
70	Romans destroy Jerusalem
80-110	Canonization of Hebrew Bible
220-552	Buddhist missions to China and Japan
304-589	Huns fragment China
325	First Ecumenical Council at Nicaea
451	Council of Chalcedon
500	Compilation of Babylonian Talmud
570-632	Muhammad

170

637	Islamic invasion of Persia
645	Taika reform—Japan takes Chinese model
650	Canonization of Qur'an
712-720	Shinto Chronicles
749	First Buddhist monastery in Tibet
762	Foundation of Baghdad
800-900	Rise of Hindu orthodoxy
966	Foundation of Cairo
1054	Mutual anathemas of Rome and Constantinople
1058-1111	Al-Ghazali
1175	First Muslim empire in India
1175-1253	Introduction of Pure Land, Zen, and Nichiren schools in Japan
1225-1274	Thomas Aquinas
1453	Ottoman Turks capture Constantinople
1492	Expulsion of Jews from Spain
1517	Luther's ninety-five theses
1526-1707	Islamic Mogul Dynasty in India
1565	Roman Catholic colony at St. Augustine
1619	Beginning of black slavery in colonial America
1654	Jewish settlement at New Amsterdam
1809-1882	Charles Darwin
1818-1883	Karl Marx
1856-1939	Sigmund Freud
1869-1948	Mahatma Gandhi
1893-1977	Mao Tse-tung
1910	Beginning of Protestant ecumenical movement
1933-1945	Nazi persecution of Jews
1948	Creation of state of Israel
1954-1956	Sixth Buddhist Council, Rangoon
1962-1965	Second Vatican Council

Glossary

agape: Christian term for self-spending love

ahimsa: Hindu nonviolence or noninjury

anthropocentrism: being pivoted on human concerns

atman: Buddhist and Hindu term for self or substantial entity

avatar: Hindu term for a manifestation of a god in earthly form

bhakta: a loving devotee of a Hindu god such as Krishna

bhakti: Hindu term for devotion

bodhisavatta: Mahayana Buddhist term for enlightened one who labors for others' salvation

Buddhanature: the wisdom-essence of all things

Caliphate: the rulership of early Islam

canon: the principal prayer of the Christian Eucharist; list of official scriptures

Ch'an: Chinese Mahayana Buddhist school stressing meditation

communion: Christian act of receiving Christ's body and blood

dharma: The teaching of the Buddha; Buddhist doctrine and truth; Hindu social theory

dharmakaya: term for the transcendental or universal body of the Buddha

dhikr ("zicker"): Muslim term for recollection or remembrance (of God)

ecumenism: largely Christian term for movement towards worldwide or transdenominational unity

enstasis: self-possession, spiritual collection of the self

eros: love that responds to beauty desireously

Eucharist: Christian sacramental meal of thanksgiving, based on Jesus' Last Supper

hadith: Muslim traditions about Muhammad

hajj: Muslim pilgrimage to Mecca

jihad: Muslim holy war

jinn: Arabic term for demon or spirit

kalpa: one of Hinduism's vast measures of time

kami: Shinto gods or spirits

karma: Hindu and Buddhist term for the moral law of cause and effect

koan: paradoxical saying used by Zen Masters to help pupils progress toward enlightenment

Koran: Muslim scripture, composed of God's revelations to Muhammad

Kuan-yin: the female form of Avalokitesvara, who became the great savior figure of much of East Asia

Maat: Egyptian goddess or notion of cosmic order

mahakaruna: Buddhist virtue of great compassion

maya: Hindu term for reality taken as so marvelous that it proves incomprehensible and unreliable for human beings

mihrab: niche in a mosque showing the direction of Mecca

mikvah: Jewish ritual bath

moksha: Hindu term for release, liberation, salvation

nirvana: Buddhist goal of liberation, salvation, or fulfillment

orders: Christian sacrament for those taking up an official church ministry

pa: Chinese term for violence, the opposite of wu-wei

passover: Jewish commemoration of the Exodus, Moses' leading the people out of bondage in Egypt

prajna: Buddhist term for wisdom

purdah: Muslim custom of veiling women

rasul: Muslim prophet or messenger

Roshi: Japanese Buddhist term for teacher or master

samadhi: Indian term for highest state of meditation or yoga

samsara: Hindu and Buddhist term for the state of continual rebirths

Shariah: the path, canon law, or general teaching of Islam

Shekinah: Jewish term for the divine presence

sheol: Jewish term for the place of the departed

Shia: sectarian Islam that opposed the Sunni orthodoxy

Shinto: native Japanese traditions centered on the kami

sila: Buddhist term for morality, the ethical precepts binding on all Buddhists (e.g., not to kill, lie, steal, fornicate, or drink intoxicants)

Sila: Eskimo deity

Sunni: majority sect of Islam

Talmud: primary source of Jewish law and rabbinic learning

Tao ("dow"): Chinese term for cosmic and moral "Way" or "Path"

Tara: Buddhist female bodhisattva or goddess especially revered in Tibet

te: Chinese term for power or virtue

theocracy: a political unit in which religious and secular authority are fused in the hands of the religious leaders

theoria: Greek term for speculative reason

T'ien: Chinese term for heaven

Torah: Jewish revelation or law

upaya: Buddhist term for "skill in means" to achieve salvation

wu-wei: Taoist notion of active not-doing

yang: Chinese principle of nature that is positive, light, and male

yin: Chinese principle of nature that is negative, dark, and female

yoga: Hindu and Buddhist term for discipline, especially that which is interior and meditative

zakat: Muslim almsgiving

zedek: Jewish term for justice

Zen: Japanese school of Buddhism that stresses meditation

zetesis: Greek term for the movement of the human spirit toward truth or God

Annotated Bibliography

1 | GENERAL TREATMENTS OF RELIGION

Carmody, Denise Lardner and Carmody, John Tully, *Ways to the Center,* 2nd ed. Belmont, Cal.: Wadsworth, 1984. A comprehensive overview stressing history and structural analysis.

Daedalus, Volume 111, Number 1 (Winter 1982). *Religion.* A collection of essays by leading scholars who try to interpret the current significance of religion, both in the United States and on the world scene.

Hall, T. William, general editor, *Introduction to the Study of Religion.* San Francisco: Harper & Row, 1978. A team of scholars from Syracuse University tackles the major conceptual topics.

Hick, John H., *Philosophy of Religion,* 3rd ed. Englewood Cliffs, N.J.: Prentice-Hall, 1983. A good survey of the main problems and concepts involved in the philosophical study of religion.

Smart, Ninian and Hecht, Richard D., eds., *Sacred Texts of the World: A Universal Anthology.* New York: Crossroad, 1982. A good collection of primary sources on all the traditions that we treat.

2 | BUDDHISM

Conze, Edward, *et al.*, eds., *Buddhist Texts Through the Ages.* New York: Harper Torchbooks, 1964. A good selection of representative primary sources, dealing with most of the major Buddhist sects.

Franck, Frederick, ed., *The Buddha Eye.* New York: Crossroad, 1982. An anthology of writings by members of the recent Kyoto school, one of the most influential modern circles of Buddhist philosophy.

King, Winston, *In the Hope of Nibbana: Theravada Buddhist Ethics.* LaSalle, Ill.: Open Court 1964. A solid study of the framework and content of Theravada ethics, both individual and social.

Rahula, Walpola, *What the Buddha Taught,* rev. ed. New York: Grove Press, 1974. A fine exposition, focusing especially on the Four Noble Truths, with selected important texts.

Robinson, Richard H., and Johnson, Willard L., *The Buddhist Religion.* Encino, Calif.: Dickenson, 1977. A comprehensive survey of Buddhist religion throughout the world.

3 | CHRISTIANITY

Carmody, Denise Lardner and John Tully, *Christianity: An Introduction.* Belmont, Ca.: Wadsworth, 1983. A basic text that offers an analysis of the Christian worldview, a succinct history, and sketches of current schools of Christian religious thought.

Carmody, John, *The Heart of the Christian Matter.* Nashville: Abingdon, 1983. An ecumenical approach that stresses Protestant prophecy, Catholic wisdom, and Orthodox worship.

Clebsch, William A., *Christianity in European History.* New York: Oxford University Press, 1979. A somewhat demanding but stimulating view, set in terms of religious studies rather than church history.

Neill, Stephen, *Jesus through Many Eyes.* Philadelphia: Fortress, 1976. A good presentation of recent New Testament scholarship that shows the distinctive theologies of the different New Testament writers.

Schmemann, Alexander, *The Historical Road of Eastern Orthodoxy.* Crestwood, N.Y.: St. Vladimir's Seminary Press, 1977. A view of the development of Orthodoxy from New Testament times, originally written for Russian Christians.

4 | HINDUISM

Basham, A. L., *The Wonder That Was India.* New York: Grove Press, 1959. A readable and comprehensive study of Indian life before the coming of the Muslims.

Hopkins, Thomas J., *The Hindu Religious Tradition.* Encino, Calif.: Dickenson, 1971. A brief and solid survey of the major religious developments.

Kinsley, David R., *Hinduism.* Englewood Cliffs, N.J.: Prentice-Hall, 1982. A brief introduction that offers a cultural perspective on Hindu history and thought.

Stanford, Anne, trans., *The Bhagavad Gita.* New York: Seabury, 1970. A fairly readable verse translation of India's most influential book.

Younger, Paul and Younger, Susanna, *Hinduism.* Niles, Ill.: Argus, 1978. A very brief, well illustrated sketch of Hindu traditions, ideas, and practices.

5 | ISLAM

Cragg, Kenneth, *The House of Islam,* 2nd ed. Encino, Calif.: Dickenson, 1975. An analysis of major topics in Islam, such as its view of God, the role of Muhammad, liturgy, and Sufism.

Donohue, John J. and Esposito, John L., eds., *Islam in Transition.* New York: Oxford University Press, 1982. Texts from Islamic commentators on recent social changes.

Faruqui, Ismaiil al, *Islam.* Niles, Ill.: Argus, 1979. A simple introduction that offers an overview of Islamic thought and practice—well illustrated.

Geertz, Clifford, *Islam Observed.* Chicago: University of Chicago Press, 1968. A brief, somewhat difficult but rewarding analysis of religious development in Morocco and Indonesia by a leading cultural anthropologist.

Rahman, Fazlur, *Islam.* Garden City, N.Y.: Doubleday, 1968. A solid, fact-filled history of Islam from Muhammad to the present.

6 | JUDAISM

Cohen, A., *Everyman's Talmud.* New York: Schocken, 1975. A topical presentation of rabbinic Judaism's main teachings, rich in quotations and details.

Heilman, Samuel C., *Synagogue Life.* Chicago: University of Chicago Press, 1976. A sociological study of the interactions among Jews at synagogue gatherings.

Neusner, Jacob, *The Life of Torah.* Encino, Calif.: Dickenson, 1974. A selection of readings that illustrate basic aspects of Jewish faith, both traditional and modern.

Neusner, Jacob, *The Way of Torah,* 2nd ed. Encino, Calif.: Dickenson, 1974. A readable introduction to Judaism that delineates its classical structure, the Torah, and the modern situation.

Zborowski, Mark, and Herzog, Elizabeth, *Life Is with People.* New York: Schocken, 1962. An absorbing portrait of *shtetl* life prior to World War II, based on interviews and personal reminiscences.

7 | TAOISM

Bush, Richard C., *Religion in China.* Niles, Ill.: Argus, 1977. A brief presentation of Chinese religion as a "stream" with several contributing "currents." Well illustrated.

Thompson, Laurence G., *The Chinese Religion: An Introduction,* 2nd ed. Encino, Calif.: Dickenson, 1975. An overview of the major components of Chinese religious culture.

Thompson, Laurence G., *The Chinese Way in Religion.* Encino, Calif.: Dickenson, 1973. A good collection of original sources that represent the span of Chinese religion.

Waley, Arthur, trans., *The Way and Its Power.* New York: Grove Press, 1958. A readable version of China's most beguiling classic.

Welch, Holmes, *Taoism: The Parting of the Way.* Boston: Beacon, 1965. A good survey of both the *Tao Te Ching* and religious Taoism.

8 | SPECIAL QUESTIONS

Auel, Jean M., *The Clan of the Cave Bear.* New York: Bantam, 1981. A persuasive novel about Neanderthal life that focuses on women's roles.

Carmody, Denise Lardner, *Feminism and Christianity: A Two-Way Reflection.* Nashville: Abingdon, 1982. A comparison of Christian and feminist insights on the four headings of sociology, ecology, psychology, and theology.

Carmody, Denise Lardner, *Women and World Religions.* Nashville: Abingdon, 1979. A survey of female images and roles in the major religious traditions that describes what being religious as a female has meant in the past and means today.

Gill, Sam D., *Beyond the Primitive: The Religions of Nonliterate Peoples.* Englewood Cliffs, N.J.: Prentice-Hall, 1982. A good theoretical orientation to the study of non-literate peoples, informed by recent cultural anthropology and laced with many examples.

Harner, Michael, *The Way of the Shaman.* San Francisco: Harper & Row, 1980. A clear presentation of the non-ordinary reality used by shamans, with many tips on how to adapt shamanic techniques to current Western life.

Neville, Robert C., *Soldier, Sage, Saint.* New York: Fordham University Press, 1978. Typological studies of some of the dominant religious personalities.

Tsunoda, Ryusaku, *et al.*, eds., *Sources of Japanese Tradition,* two volumes, New York: Comumbia University Press, 1964. A good anthology of important texts throughout Japanese religious history.

Index

179